MY
CRYSTAL BALL

The Invisible Side of Parkinson's

CRYSTAL BALL

The Invisible Side of Parkinson's

DEBORAH WILTON MCLOUGHLIN

My Crystal Ball: The Invisible Side of Parkinson's

Cover and Interior Design: Indigo Design, Inc.

designbyindigo.com

ISBN 978-0-692-41987-8

Printed in the U.S.A.

To my husband Bernie and to Ryan my son: you could always make me laugh, and as long as there is laughter there is HOPE

And to all the people who are working so hard to find the cures for these diseases, THANK YOU

May our paths cross soon

TABLE OF CONTENTS

FOREWORD

My *Crystal Ball* describes a patient's personal outlook on her walk with Parkinson's Disease and its impact on her daily life. It is very informative, and I strongly recommend it for its potential to add to the intrinsic resources of anyone diagnosed with the condition. Furthermore, any physician or other professional who is involved in the care of Parkinson's patients should also lend a thoughtful mind and an attentive ear to what Deborah McLoughlin has to say.

Her book provides insight on some impactful aspects of this condition, mostly psychological, that are easily overlooked during office evaluations. If the patient, care provider(s), physician, and family members are aware of the defensive "glossing-over" that occurs as an attempt to avoid the doom and gloom that may be involved in conversations concerning progression of the disease, there might be interventions enacted to "take control" before accumulated and ignored problems turn into a runaway train.

Sanjay P. Rathi, M.D.
Neurology, Movement Disorders and Dystonia , LLC.

PREFACE

None of us can predict the future. None of us knows the crown of thorns or bed of roses that will define our lives. But those of us living with a neurodegenerative disease—be it Alzheimer's, MS, ALS or, in my case, Parkinson's—have been given a glimpse into a crystal ball showing us a future we neither anticipated nor wanted nor planned for, a future that would consume every facet of our lives, as well as the lives of our families.

If you have been diagnosed with Parkinson's recently, I am not going to sugarcoat this: it stinks. Yet, you can do many things to make your days easier. First, keep in mind that Parkinson's is not a death sentence. Many people have lived their lives extremely well while dealing with the various effects of the disease. When you can't do a particular thing anymore, you learn to compensate. You come to rely on others and to ask for help, and friends and loved ones are more than happy to provide what you need. Actually, most want to help in any way they can, but they do not know what to offer you unless you tell them what you need.

My Crystal Ball is intended to orient those who have been diagnosed with debilitating diseases such as Parkinson's, and for their families and loved ones. I want to quiet their fears as they begin their journey into the future together. I also want doctors to see the other side of Parkinson's, the invisible side, so they will know what their patients are going through.

Mine is just one story, one reflection in the crystal ball.

INTRODUCTION

I always wanted to be an artist and a writer, even before I knew what they were called. My mother swore I was born with a crayon in each hand. My early attempts at artistry were not merely refrigerator-worthy; they were front-door-worthy. The front door was my personal art gallery, filled with witches and pumpkins at Halloween, and Santas and snowmen at Christmas. My mom saved my creations from year to year until I created a replacement or they had been bleached out by the sun.

Writing was my next love. My kindergarten classroom was next to the first-grade classroom. While we kinders were just learning our letters, the first graders were putting those letters together to make sentences. The blue-lined yellow paper that hung outside their classroom for all the school to see fascinated me. They were covered with words I could not recognize; yet I was thrilled to know what awaited me at the next level.

As I grew, I recognized that authors could use their words to transport readers to the heavens and beyond, and bring them back to middle earth again. Words introduce you to people you do not want to let go of when the last word of the last chapter is read. Words can be hurtful and mean or they can comfort someone who is broken. Words can start wars and bring them to an end. This was powerful stuff, and I wanted to harness this power. By the time I was a teenager, my desire to become a writer was all-consuming. I vividly remember lying in bed at night when the house was quiet and feeling, really feeling, that writing was my destiny, that someday my name would be on the cover of a real book. During high school, I was the dreamer, the artist, the writer. These interests were not nurtured or favored in the math and science curriculum of my college-prep high school. I won several awards for my works of art and short stories, but I will always remember that these awards were not as valued or praised as those given in the areas of science or math.

In junior year, I tried out for the school paper. At the meeting announcing the newspaper staff, at least six names were called out for the reporting slots. Mine was not called. Four more names were called to be the section editors. Again my name was not called. Was I such a horrible writer? I wanted to run out of the room and cry. Then, the advisor announced the slot of assistant editor. Me! It was one of the most wonderful moments of my high school life. Even after all these years, I can still feel what I felt on that day. I did well and was promoted to editor-in-chief for my senior year. I won awards for my school paper, especially for the editorial page, something that had never before been accomplished.

I had one wonderful English teacher who mentored me. I could write short stories, but an entire novel? Not a chance. When I was probably ten, I started writing one in the Hardy Boys/Nancy Drew genre, but couldn't think up a good mystery, let alone solve it. My teacher, as well as almost any writer, will tell you to write about what you know if you want to write effectively. I never thought I would write a book about an ugly disease that is slowly taking over my life. I didn't think my life would take this turn, and I certainly wouldn't have chosen it, but it has given me a good deal to write about.

When I was first diagnosed with Parkinson's, I felt lost and alone. And frightened. I knew no one who had the disease, and I wasn't exactly sure what it was. I knew about the tremors, but I knew there must be a lot more to it. I had observed that the word Parkinson's was spoken in a whisper, like a terrible secret and embarrassment for the person who had it. I have always believed that bad things happen for a reason, that we aren't given something we can't handle and therefore that we have a responsibility to make the bad things in our lives right. But Parkinson's is a big bad thing, and for me, it is something I will come to know all too well.

MY CRYSTAL BALL

If you were given the chance to gaze into a crystal ball and see your future, would you? I never thought I would. Maybe that's because I like surprises—good surprises. But what if your future wasn't going to be filled with good surprises? Maybe you wouldn't want to know what lay in store for you. Especially if it was something you felt you couldn't handle or change.

Until I was diagnosed with PD, my life was idyllic. I married a successful, handsome man. (And let's not forget witty; he is Irish, after all.) We had a talented and drop-dead gorgeous son who graduated magna cum laude from Berklee College of Music. Before my son was born in 1988, I'd had a moderately successful career in HR at the Southern New England Telephone Company, but it was just a job. Not a career. When my son was born, I couldn't get out of there fast enough. I enjoyed every minute I spent with him, counting the blades of grass on our front lawn as we waited for Daddy to come home or visiting construction sites where he was mesmerized by the dance of the heavy equipment.

I saw my mother in me as I played kid games, like Hide and Seek, and Tag. I wished that he could stay little forever, but I was also curious to see the man he would grow up to be. I always regret that my husband and I didn't have more children. We tried. I didn't want my son to be alone. I wanted him to share memories with a brother or sister, to grow up with someone who has the same history, someone who remembers the little things you have forgotten that only a sibling would know. I wanted him to have the same rich relationship with a brother or a sister as I had with my brother. I wanted him to have someone to talk to about his aging parents, someone to share the burden of making the financial, medical, and other arrangements that elderly parents always need. It was not to be.

When my son got older and wanted to play with his friends from school, I sadly turned away from being a big part of his life, knowing that he would devote the next six years or so to his friends and growing up. Instead, I turned to my first loves: art and writing. My life was turning out just the way I wanted. I had no idea what was waiting to greet me in the future. If God wanted to grab my attention, He sure got it.

I first gazed into that crystal ball, quite unwillingly, when I was diagnosed with Parkinson's disease. I was forty-nine years old. My first thoughts were probably similar to those of any person given a turn-your-world-upside-down, where-did-this-come-from diagnosis: I had a teenage son; would I be able to attend my son's graduation, his wedding? Would I be able to hold my grandchildren? Reality kicked in for a moment, and the gravity of PD struck me with a barrage of alarming thoughts: Would I be able to stay in my home? Would I be able to take care of myself and my husband? Would we have to find someone to take care of me? Would I be able to continue painting and playing the piano, both of which require a steady hand?

What I glimpsed in that crystal ball smashed my once certain and promising future into pieces, just like I wanted to do to that crystal ball. And what about the financial ramifications of the disease? They could be as debilitating as the disease itself. Would this demon following us for the rest of our lives jeopardize all our hard work and savings over the years?

When Parkinson's raised its ugly head at an all-too-early stage in my life, like Michael J. Fox, I turned to the internet, searching for answers to my faltering step and unsteady hand. I read the list of symptoms, which included shaky handwriting, soft speech, changes in walking, rigidity, and trouble sleeping. I was alarmed that of the ten or so symptoms listed, I was experiencing eight. And for the first time in my life, staring at the words on my computer screen, I was faced with the possibility of a major, life-altering illness.

Like my friend Michael J. Fox, despite having the symptoms, I zeroed in on the phrase "usually affects people over sixty." I had a long way to go before I turned sixty. For a moment, relief flooded me. There had to be other conditions with similar symptoms. Maybe I had been misdiagnosed! No one in my family had Parkinson's disease. Where had it come from? Finally, I asked the same question that everyone asks: "Dear God, what have I done that was so bad I have to suffer with this?"

I hoped to find a way to deal with the unexpected path my life had taken. What I discovered is this: PD is an alienating disease. You fold into yourself and become smaller and smaller until you cannot be seen. It makes you want to sit and watch the world go by, be a non-participant. I vowed I would keep participating.

I learned that there are no answers, just more questions, the answers to some of which I didn't want to hear. I was scared, scared every time I saw pictures of Muhammad Ali or the late Pope John Paul II in what is called the "final stage of the disease." I can't think of a more horrible description. All I could do was pray even more earnestly and hold tight to the hope that this life-stealing disease would be wiped out in my lifetime.

That's when I turned to my words. I started blogging as a way to cope with my shocking diagnosis and to face my demons head-on. I wanted to hear how other people coped with such a devastating prognosis. As well, I thought others might be interested in following the emotions that accompany a person living with Parkinson's. All I could think of was how to use those powerful words I eagerly learned as a child to shine a brighter light on a disease that was once considered an old person's disease, but is now beginning to affect greater numbers of younger people, many while still in their forties. I would not become a non-participant. I would speak up for those whose voices have been silenced by Parkinson's. I would voice my hope that researchers will shortly come up with something—if not a cure, then something to stop or slow down its progression. I would share with other sufferers the practical and sometimes impractical things we can do to make our lives easier.

When I started my blog, I wanted to remain anonymous. The internet was the perfect place for my story, and I would be able to maintain my cover. I told no one for a long time that I was Crystal Ball, the name I used for my blog. I hoped that the power of social media would reveal someone out there who had beat Parkinson's into submission, someone who would give me the hope that I could live with it by making a few adjustments along the way. Yes, I admit I wanted to find someone who would give me a big dash of hope by telling me Parkinson's could be conquered. I wanted to find new ways that other people were using to deal with this monster. Ultimately, I wanted to destroy it.

Initially, I didn't want to discuss the physical aspects of the disease; I wanted to chronicle the emotional side of a disease that slowly steals your identity. I wanted to write about how I cope when I wake up in the morning and find that yet another piece of me was stolen during the night. I thought it might lead to an interesting study. If others joined me in sharing our common experiences, I thought we might learn from each other as we prepare for the future. So, I turned to the internet as a way to make myself heard.

The technology-challenged among us should not be allowed to touch cell phones or computers. I know this first hand. After much frustration with technology and constantly losing posts (some of my best writing is lost forever in never-never land), I published my first post in December 2011. I didn't know the reaction I would receive.

I wanted to communicate how someone given such a diagnosis could continue to enjoy their lives. Because I asked the question, "If you could look into a crystal ball and see your future, would you?" I named my blog Crystal Ball and Parkinson's. Initially I only wrote once or twice a month, but then really got into it until I was consumed with writing. Every morning, the first thing I did was look to see how many hits I had gotten on the previous day. When I put the blog on hold to write this book, I had over 12,000 hits, but honestly, I didn't really know what hits were, whether they represented individuals reading my words or were some kind of technical way that my blog was being, in effect, read by a computer.

In the end, I was disappointed. I had hoped to engage my "readers" in conversation about PD, but got very few takers.

From the blog, this book was born. In these pages, I have used my words to laugh and cry, to come to terms with my life, and, I hope, to comfort others who are experiencing the hardships of Parkinson's. I have opened my soul to the world, something I never thought I could do. I have come to realize that we all have challenges. Parkinson's is just one. Not everyone has a scary diagnosis, but we all have life challenges because we are alive. Selling a beloved home, struggling with finances and ill health, helping the kids through college, and growing older impact us all, whatever other burdens we carry. Life happens. It doesn't stop for PD or cancer or any disease.

I would like to make a difference in someone's life, to feel that I am living my life for a purpose. I would like to make someone who has forgotten how to laugh, laugh again. To comfort someone newly diagnosed by showing that Parkinson's is manageable. To gain reassurances from those who have been here before me and pass on those same reassurances to others.

Writing a book is a big item on my bucket list. It is my personal victory, a goal I set when I was a child. I will wait to check it off when the first copy is in my hands. I wrote it to prove to myself that, even with PD, I can still accomplish a goal I believed I would never reach even before I was diagnosed.

As I was working on this manuscript, Hubby asked if I was going to talk about all the things I still do, even with PD. "Don't you want to show people what you have accomplished? Even with the PD? What they can still do? Like, you still travel; you paint; you mentor a high school student. You swim, walk, and exercise."

I thought about it. I decided that I want this book to be real. I want it to be balanced. That is, I want it to include both my optimism and the realities I deal with, including my imperfections and fears and other ugly stuff. I want to let people know, if they don't already, what a horrible disease Parkinson's is. Some days, it takes every ounce of my strength to get out of bed in the mornings. There are days when I feel really good, just like my old self. And then the following day, I can feel my muscles struggling to hold me up. PD takes and takes. This good days/bad days scenario is a constant reminder of what it is like to feel good and whole again, but only for a little while. Inevitably, like the mythological phoenix, PD rises from the ashes, pounces on me, and takes everything back, leaving me with only a wisp, a shadow, and the memories of what I used to do so easily.

THE FIRST MONTHS:
ACCEPTING THE DIAGNOSIS

I think it is important, and I hope interesting, for you to know what was happening to me just before and after my diagnosis of Parkinson's.

My symptoms developed slowly. About two years before I knew that Parkinson's was gnawing at my brain, I had some minor symptoms I considered no more than a prelude to crossing the line into my fifties. My fifties didn't scare me. I exercised regularly and ate properly (cookies are a valid food group, are they not?). I was ready for another fifty years of travel, parties, and time spent with family and friends. The symptoms I was experiencing were happening more often; they were little things. For example, frequently when I reached out to put a glass on a table, my hand shook. My mom had a benign tremor, and that is what I assumed I had.

A couple of years later, I noticed that my arm wasn't swinging as naturally as it should when I walked; instead, it just hung at my side. I had been in a serious automobile crash and, among other things, my arm had been broken. I thought that might be the reason. I was really grabbing at straws with that one. Casually, I mentioned it to my doctor, who recommended I see a neurologist. You know how you sometimes get a gut feeling that something is wrong? That is what I felt.

The neurologist sent me for a CAT scan to rule out the possibility of a stroke. A few days later, I was sitting in his office, waiting to hear the results. Parkinson's had been mentioned as a possibility during my first visit, but I was certain it had to be something else. So, I will never forget what the neurologist said: "I have good news and good news. You did not have a stroke, and what you have is treatable." I breathed with relief. And then he said that the diagnosis was Parkinson's. Actually, he called it *Parkinsonism.* I'm not sure why, but it made me feel better. It wasn't full-blown Parkinson's. Even so, after that, Parkinson's was the word I went to bed with every night and woke up with first thing in the morning. Yes, I knew there were medications to control the symptoms, but was it treatable? As in *curable?* Did the doctor know something I didn't?

It is interesting to notice the different ways people react to bad news. I went home, lay on the bed, and cried. Then I got up, dried my eyes, wiped off my remaining mascara, and cried some more. That was okay, I decided, because crying can be part of the acceptance and healing process.

My husband, on the other hand, got angry. But who was he angry at? At the doctors? At the disease? At God? At me? I knew my husband, and I knew he was terribly upset, not at me, but at the world in general. He was angry that our future had been taken away with one word. After forty years of marriage, I can tell when he is really angry and upset because he throws things. Well, to be honest, he doesn't really throw things, but he sure does put them down vigorously. If there were a wall in front of him when he gets frustrated with something minor that isn't going right, I believe he would actually punch a hole through it.

He is the quintessential type A personality. He has the bills in the envelopes and paid before the mail carrier reaches the other end of the block. He is the practical one of us, the left-brained person who thinks analytically. I am sure he saw all the plans for our future smashed to pieces. At that point, even though we were husband and wife and should be sharing everything with each other and consoling each other, I could not let him see me weak and crying. He had to believe I could handle this until something better comes along to treat it, that I still hold out hope for a cure in my lifetime. I know the head doctors would probably refute this approach, but I didn't want someone else to hurt so much because of me. I knew we were both in denial, and if I looked like I had PD, then we couldn't lie to ourselves anymore. Just give us this moment, I thought, brief as it may be, to be whole again. I got out of bed again and dried my eyes. I told myself I could handle it.

I sometimes think that the spouse who does not have the disease imagines it is worse than it is. It is magnified in their eyes and made all the more horrible because the person they love has to fight it mostly alone. On the afternoon of my diagnosis, I irrationally felt that it was my fault I got PD. I felt I had really screwed things up for our future. I made up my mind that I could handle it as it was and that there would be a cure for me, soon. I reminded myself that right at that very moment, researchers were out there working on it. I just knew they were getting closer.

Until they crack that final test tube, however, the "cure" is called *Hope,* and it is one of the strongest meds I know. Hope is what I clung to in the weeks and years following the news, and I still cling to it today. Throw in a little denial and probably stupidity, and you can get on with your life until the next challenge is thrown your way.

THE OPTIMIST

I am the eternal optimist. I have always seen the glass as half full. Shortly after I discovered what life had in store for me, I saw a news clip about an older couple. The husband had just been diagnosed with Alzheimer's. I wish I could quote the wife verbatim. She said what most everyone says, a version of, "Live each day to the fullest." But she said it poetically and so beautifully. She added that since none of us has a crystal ball, we don't know what tomorrow will bring. "Why waste this beautiful day thinking and worrying about what may never happen. You get up each day and get on with your life and don't waste a minute of it. Grab it with both hands and shake it for all it's worth and believe that many more good days will follow."

After the doctor's visit in which I received my diagnosis, I had a feeling that something else was wrong; not necessarily with me, but I felt more bad news was coming my way. I had always believed that life evens out eventually, that our good days equal our bad days, if you know what I mean. I had been having many good days before this one, so I wondered if this was the beginning of my bad days. In a sense, it was.

I soon discovered that my father had been diagnosed with pancreatic cancer, and he died very quickly thereafter. I was left to care for my mother and my two aunts, her unmarried sisters. Affectionately known as the Golden Girls, they had been dependent on my father to take them shopping and to doctor's visits. He had been their grass-mower and snow-shoveler, their chauffeur and errand-runner. At that time, their needs were basic care, grocery shopping, meal preparation, and transportation to doctor visits.

I became the provider of that care. We made quite the scene, climbing in and out of my SUV: one with a cane, one with a walker, and one with a wheeled tank of oxygen that probably weighed more than she did. Whenever there was a reason to go out, they all went out, and that reason was almost always a doctor visit. Never mind that they all went to different doctors for different reasons. Anyone's appointment was up for grabs, a chance to go out. I regularly loaded up the SUV with the three of them and their equipment and took off, rain, shine, or snow. The weather rarely cooperated. I sometimes suggested that just the one with the appointment should go while the others stayed home, but I would arrive, and there the three of them would be, all wrapped up in their coats or sweaters. Waiting for me.

I think my new responsibilities kept me going and slowed down my symptoms. I had too many other responsibilities to be bothered with my own worries. Probably the worst part was that I felt I couldn't tell anyone about my diagnosis, because if the news got back to the Golden Girls, they would be devastated.

Girls' Night Out

The fifties. I have always considered our fifties the most difficult decade to live through; coming through it unscathed makes you one of the truly lucky ones. When I turned fifty, I had been diagnosed with PD for a year. PD certainly did not make my fifties any easier.

When you enter your fifties, chances are your parents are in their seventies or eighties. Their bodies are beginning to fail them, and they need extra help with the shopping or laundry and an additional ear at their doctor appointments. So, hopefully, you try to help them cope while dealing with your own problems. And, if you do not live near them, guilt and worry set in.

If you waited to have kids, as many people do nowadays, their school and other activities pull at your time, as well. Older kids may need your financial help or emotional support or, God forbid, a room to come home to.

Then there is you. Besides being in the middle of this sandwich, you are experiencing the onset of the so-called golden years, and all these responsibilities make them, well, not so golden. You start reading the obituaries and recognize too many faces, just like your parents used to do while you laughed at them all the while, uneasily suspecting that you would someday be doing the same.

After I turned fifty, I noticed that every time the phone rang, it was bad news, sometimes horrible news. I decided my friends and I needed some lightening up. I am a firm believer in the healing power of laughter, the hearty kind of laughter that makes your eyes water, your make-up run, and your whole body double over. Therefore, one day about five years ago, perhaps not long after one of those alarming phone calls, I decided to organize a regular Girls' Night Out at my house. The rule was that we must leave our problems at the door. We could spend only ten minutes on our troubles, and then we had to shoo them away. Unfortunately, we had to pick them up again when the evening was over, but we didn't deal with that. I just wanted us to laugh all evening, just laugh and laugh and laugh, and that's what we do. We have been meeting for several years. We look forward to our time to socialize and nosh and maybe forget the ties that bind us to our problems for at least an evening. Sometimes, we go to the movies. Often, we just sit around and chat. These women were already my friends when I formed the group, and now they are my dearest friends. We are there for each other, and we all know it.

Ladies, you know who you are. We share the burdens as well as the glories of our lives. Some of us have been lucky enough to retire and travel or pursue a new hobby or direction. Now, the grandbabies are starting to arrive, and who can resist a baby?

We celebrate the good times with each other and console each other in the bad. We know who can work with the computer, and Marianne is in constant demand (at least from me). If you want a fantastic dinner, you call Jeanne. A fantastic pasta sauce? Call Marianne again. Kathy knows all about flowers and gardening, and the other Debbie is just plain fun to have around. Accounting questions, call Anne. Connie is our nature girl. She has been known to rescue a baby bird from becoming a cat's meal, and then take it home and nurse it back to health. And I can't forget Barbara, who knows where to get the best kielbasa in the state. Then, there is Janice. Because of a bad thing that happened, I was introduced to her, and she became one of my dearest friends.

My friends and I periodically reevaluate what is important to us. We realize that we are the only ones who can create change in our lives. If we can laugh at ourselves, too, all the better.

KEEPING AND SHARING SECRETS

I have learned a lot about human nature and my own peculiarities in the years since I was diagnosed. I learned that most people cannot keep a secret, and Parkinson's was one secret that I could never share with anyone—or at least not until I was certain the Golden Girls would never hear about it. I didn't even tell my brother, and I know he would have kept it to himself, but I didn't want to put him under that pressure.

I also verified that Hubby cannot keep a secret, but I knew that already. Early on, he told a friend who told a friend. I was mad as hell. This was my secret to be told on my timeline. It took me a while to forgive him, but eventually I realized that he probably needed someone to talk to besides me. So, for the record, once you tell someone a secret, once you share something with a second person, you can be sure it is not a secret anymore.

Why was I so determined not to let anyone know? In my mind, I believed my disease diminished me as a person. I was broken. Damaged goods. And I couldn't help believing that it was somehow my fault that I got PD. Should I have eaten more veggies? Less candy? More coffee? Should I have refused to have the house treated for ants?

So what do you do? How do you introduce people to the personal demons you carry with you twenty-four hours a day? It doesn't quite fit into normal chat. "Oh, hi. Cute shoes. By the way, I have Parkinson's." I find it difficult to say those words out loud. Hearing myself say them makes the disease more real to me.

Maybe this was why I had pretty much kept myself in the closet for almost ten years, not even telling close family members. Most people knew something was wrong, but they were kind enough to respect my privacy. Most did not comment when I had a difficult time getting up from a chair or walking, which are the two areas most affected by the PD. They helped me silently, quick to offer an arm or hand when they sensed I needed it.

How did I finally come out of the closet? Slowly. I started by blabbing it on the internet in a blog, but wrapped in the cloak of anonymity. I didn't identify myself. Initially, I didn't tell my friends about the blog, and it was not the way I wanted to tell my friends, anyway. That was something I felt I should do in person.

I discovered there are various ways of handling this. For example, I met a woman I hadn't seen in a long time, and the first thing she told me was that she had been diagnosed with cancer. I can hear her words still: "Oh, hi, Debbie…I have cancer." If I hadn't known about it already, I would have been speechless. Her blunt approach is not my style, but it is an option.

It is more my style to wait until we are saying our goodbyes and then drop the "P Bomb." Responses from friends and family covered a range of reactions. Usually, when I tell someone, they are literally speechless, and then comes the awkward silence, the deafening silence. I told one friend who was advising us about something or other, and he looked blown away. No one quite knows what to say, so they stumble with words for a while and then give me the old, "Well, there is a lot of research on this and blah, blah, blah." That is the most common response. I know it hits them hard, so I really don't mind if they don't say anything. The news comes out of nowhere, and they have to process that it's me, it's a horrible disease, and I am too young for this. Some cried. Even big, strong macho men got the sniffles, while others swore and were angry that this could happen.

When you are in the position of responding, you don't have to say anything. A warm hug will do. The one mistake I made, and I am sure my leader, Janice, has forgiven me, was to announce it to my coworkers at the end of a meeting. I had been stumbling around the issue for a while. It was probably more noticeable to me than to them. I am sure they just attributed it to another approaching birthday and feeling that they were piling up too darn fast. I had planned to tell them all at once, but people had been missing at previous meetings or other people were visiting. Finally, I announced it at a meeting when we were covering new business.

Silence. And tears. And my poor Janice was taken by surprise. I had told her previously about the PD, so she knew I was living with it. She just didn't know I would announce it without warning. I should have told her in advance, but I was so caught up in the timing and nervous about telling everyone at once that I guess I wasn't thinking clearly. To her credit, and she knows she will have my respect and friendship forever, she gave a knowledgeable description of my situation and said it should not impact anything I was involved in at work. I would continue my work life as usual. End of story. And to their credit, my coworkers treated me just as they had before, except they wouldn't allow me to carry heavy boxes. Because I was working, I felt I had to push myself to get going and strove not to let my PD show. I strove hard to make the PD invisible.

Ten years have passed since that awful word filled my head, and still no cure has been found for the millions of us fighting this battle. I can honestly say I can't complain about my life during those ten years. Sure, I do things a bit more slowly and I tire easily. Sometimes, I shuffle my feet because it feels like my legs are too heavy to pick up, but if I never get any worse than I am now, I could live with this.

And what has this diagnosis done to my husband and family? Parkinson's: one little word changed everything, caused us to face questions we had not anticipated facing until much later. Do we sell the house before we are really ready? Do we book travel plans not knowing if I will be able to walk in a year? Parkinson's turned our lives upside-down. And now my family would have to live with my diagnosis. When my mother told me she had macular degeneration and was going blind, I had to live with that information, and I worried about her constantly. I didn't want the people I love to have PD lurking in the back of their minds when it comes to making life choices. I didn't want people staring at me, talking in whispers to their friends, looking for the tremors that are a sign of the disease. I didn't want a disease to define me. I didn't want to be known as the person with the PD. Boy, had I screwed this one up!

Parkinson's Disease

Parkinson's is a disease that affects the central nervous system, causing movement and coordination issues; it is caused by damage to dopamine-producing nerve cells that are gradually dying off in the patient's brain. Researchers have not yet determined why these cells are dying, but they suspect it is likely due to genetic and environmental factors. Most people are diagnosed after age sixty, but doctors are seeing more and more cases in younger patients. While great progress has been made, scientists don't really understand the cause of PD and, although more and stronger medicines have been developed and many more are hopefully on the way, currently, the progression of this illness cannot be stopped.

PD is diagnosed by observation of the patient's actions and symptoms, which usually include slowness of movement, stiffness, balance issues, and tremor. Other symptoms can include "freezing" when walking, vivid dreams, and small, illegible handwriting. Some lose their sense of smell, and this can be used as a diagnostic tool in assessing patients. Researchers' also believe Parkinson's affects everyone differently as to the types of symptoms a patient has or how rapidly the disease progresses. Along with physical changes, emotional and mental issues must be considered. Depression is common, as well as anxiety, lack of ability to concentrate, and memory issues. Parkinson's itself is not a death sentence. People generally don't die from the disease; instead, they die from falls or choking as a result of the condition.

There are many ways to make living life with Parkinson's easier, using medications, exercise, and equipment to enable the patient to get around on his or her own. People from all walks of life have been impacted by this disease, including Michael J. Fox, the late Pope John Paul II, Muhammad Ali, former US Attorney General Janet Reno, singer Linda Ronstadt, and Robin Williams. Some believe that Hitler showed signs of Parkinson's.

Let me tell you what it physically feels like to have this disease. When you want to move, your body feels like it weighs a ton, and you do not have the strength to pick up your arms or legs. You may feel that your legs are not strong enough to support your weight, and this creates the characteristic shuffle. If you have ever had a broken bone in which they had to stabilize a moving joint, such as an elbow or shoulder, you know that after not using the muscles involved for several months, they start to atrophy and freeze, and it becomes difficult to use the joint until physical therapy frees it up.

There are four stages to the disease, but I do not care to know what they are at this point. I want to live my life the best way I can without having the image of the next phase looming over me.

Knowledge Is Power

Funny, but in the last chapter I said I didn't want to know about the stages and where PD will take me. That was my denial. Actually, knowledge is power because the more you know about something, the better you can make decisions. You need information to buy the right car, to attend the right college, and to choose a career. And if you have a medical condition, you want to know where, why, and how you were so lucky—and how you can get rid of it.

I have a very dear friend who was struggling with a diagnosis of breast cancer at around the same time I was beginning to tell people I had Parkinson's. She was the first person I told outside of my family. Marianne had gone about learning everything she could about her cancer. She researched everything from diet to different meds and surgeries. She wanted to be fully informed about her choices and the doctor's approach to her illness. I have a vision of her, sitting in bed, blanket over her head, researching her illness, her laptop emitting a muted light as her husband sleeps soundly by her side. I spoke to her at length one day, and I have to say that I wish she were my advocate. She probably has more knowledge about her disease than anybody else, and she continues to keep informed of advances in the area.

My approach was nearly the opposite. I listened to my doctor and placed all my faith in him. I was impressed by his knowledge of the disease and his desire to do the best he could for his patients. Of course, I read the books and pamphlets, but they were too complicated; they were all about dopamine antagonists and offered nothing in the way of a long-term cure. There was not much on slowing its progression. You address the symptom that is yelling the loudest to get your attention by experimenting with different types of meds and exercise, and whatever else is available, so you can tell it to shut up.

Marianne has completely changed her life: she goes to the gym almost every day and has modified her diet to avoid meat and other products deemed not the best for her form of cancer. And she doesn't waiver from this routine, at all. I am glad to say it has been six years since her diagnosis, and she looks wonderful and is full of energy. When I asked her how she could be so strict with herself, she simply said, "What choice do I have? All of us will be asked to deal with something in our lives, and we do the best we can." She is truly a strong, remarkable woman.

So, my dear friend may have inspired me to get off my rear and become more knowledgeable about my illness. To take charge of it. To own it. (Yet, I will gladly sell it to the highest bidder!)

The thing is, Parkinson's is so complicated. A short while ago, I started getting somewhat lightheaded when I stood up. It's not the sudden, passing thing that most everybody experiences occasionally, but a deep light-headedness that makes me feel I am in a vacuum and can only vaguely hear people talking around me. It feels like all my energy falls to my feet; my body gets heavy. It is an awful feeling. On two occasions, I actually passed out. Is this related to the Parkinson's, or is it a whole new area to explore?

My neurologist, Dr. Rathi, told me to call my cardiologist, who said I was perfect. I saw Dr. Rathi again, and he declared me perfect, also. Dr. Rathi tells me it is not the pills I have been popping for the last twelve years, nor is there any known interaction among them that would cause this symptom, so I am lost—and frankly, scared. What is going on in my head? Is it the heat, dehydration, or something more sinister? I wish I could get all my docs to sit around my kitchen table. I will provide the chocolate chip cookies while they share their knowledge and compare notes about me, because I feel like no one person can put all the pieces together. Medicine has become too complicated. I'm remembering a cardiologist I went to once. He asked about the meds I was taking, and when I said I only took meds for Parkinson's, he gruffly said he didn't care about my other meds. Do I have to say that he was not my doctor by the end of that appointment?

Too many docs these days specialize in one area, but don't know much about anything else. I can understand that; medicine has gotten very complicated, and one person can't know it all. But, where does that leave the patient? Where does it leave me?

Okay, since it seems to be up to me, I believe these spells are related to the meds I'm taking. The dizziness and fainting were part of my very own Perfect Storm. It was hot on the occasions it happened, I was probably dehydrated, and one of the meds should have been taken immediately before climbing into bed instead of an hour before bedtime, as I had been taking it. Probably it was leading me to the land of almost-asleep. I fell asleep in a chair, woke up groggy, and went upstairs, becoming light-headed in the process. Perhaps my blood pressure, which is very low to begin with, dropped too low, too fast. Therefore, I am experimenting with taking the med at a different time, and hopefully it will solve this ugly symptom. Poor Hubby had to pick me up off the floor twice and is now constantly tracking my whereabouts to make sure I don't fall.

I understand. I did the same thing to him when, at age sixty, he decided to paint our two-story house—by himself. My finger hovered above 911 all that time.

I am so sorry I am putting him through this, but what can I do? I promise I will be careful.

THE STUDY

At my second visit to a neurologist (not Dr. Rathi) just after I was first diagnosed with PD, the doctor told me about a local study to test the efficacy of a new drug that held a lot of promise, if not to stop the disease in its tracks, then at least to slow down its progression. If this might be a cure for Parkinson's, I wanted in on it. I jumped at a chance to be a guinea pig and get my hands on any new drug before anyone else.

The study was taking place in New Haven, Connecticut, just a short distance from where we lived. It was being conducted by the research group IND (Institute for Neurodegenerative Disorders). It would take a one-hour visit every three months. And free parking and food were provided. How could I lose?

Well, there was a downside. I had to take four huge horse pills four times a day in addition to my normal meds and drink a horrible iodine concoction at least once a year to protect my thyroid from the chemical needed to perform a brain scan. FYI, iodine tastes worse than it smells. I don't recommend it.

The study was a double-blind study, meaning neither the researchers nor the volunteers knew who was getting the actual study drug and who was taking the placebo. People from all over the country were participating, and we all shared our war stories and speculations about where we thought Parkinson's disease originated. We knew that it might be linked to chemicals, but the medical researchers could not prove it. If they did, it might be easier to treat. If they did, they might be closer to an answer. We all thought one would be forthcoming after the trial's findings were known. We all thought that the new med was working. After taking it for about five weeks, most people felt better. Even before I joined the study, my symptoms were almost nonexistent except to the trained eye. I was experiencing no tremors and no freezing. There was just my arm not swinging properly and a slight change in the way I walked.

The study went on for maybe two years before they announced their findings. Actually, it was cancelled because they had found no overwhelming or even promising difference in results from the drugs already in use. We were terribly disappointed. This was supposed to be the most promising new medicine to come along in a while. And I don't care what they concluded, because it did make us feel better. I was grateful to at least be one of the guinea pigs who received the real medication. Maybe it was the placebo effect, but every time I try to explain the unusually slow advancement and my mild symptoms so far into my diagnosis, I think of that drug. If I had not participated and received it, I would be worse off than I am. I believe that drug worked for me, and that's all I need to know.

INDEPENDENCE DAY

I was born on the Fourth of July. Independence Day. It is a great day to be born. Most people get to take the day off. There are picnics and fireworks. It is summer, and everyone is happy. Maybe being born on the Fourth of July is what makes me so patriotic and independent. Slowly, however, my independence is being eroded by the demon called Parkinson's, but I must take some of the blame for letting it.

Parkinson's disease: I was forty-nine when I first heard those words applied to me. Unlike some people, I wasn't pleased or relieved that my symptoms had finally been given a name. On July 4th, 2013, I started the journey into my sixties. That fact is scary enough, even without the Parkinson's diagnosis. I don't feel sixty. I don't think I act like someone who is sixty. I sure hope I don't look sixty. But, there it is. I had hoped for a cure, by now. Actually, at the time of my diagnosis, so many positive things were coming out of research that I fully expected a cure would be found shortly. So here I sit, preparing to celebrate another birthday without the one present I want most: relief from the monster of Parkinson's disease.

Yes, my independence is slowly eroding. And isn't my husband's independence also being stolen? I don't want to be a clingy wife. I don't want to follow my husband around, and I am sure he doesn't want me everywhere he goes. Understandable, but I am so much more comfortable holding his arm. There will be many things I can do today, but won't be able to accomplish tomorrow—even when I am holding his hand. Things that should have warning lights blinking: "Keep Away! Not recommended for PD patients!"

One of the worst side effects of this disease is loss of balance; I could easily tumble down a flight of stairs and break my neck. I fear going shopping in an expensive store and falling into a display of breakables. To prevent this casualty, I usually carry a cane, and the cane steadies me. (I will tell you more about that in a little bit.) I can't do dark places, like a movie theater, because they completely throw off my equilibrium. Even in my own home, I need to keep a light on so I do not get lost in the dark. Because I am so afraid of falling, I hold onto the wall and let it guide me to my bedroom door. At those times, I need someone's arm to hold. And pushing and shoving crowds are not my thing because of this proclivity to fall. Even going out to dinner has its dangers. If I sit too long at the table, I get stiff and find it difficult to get up, which means that before dinner is over, I am worrying about how to best stand up without everybody seeing me stagger. I am sure more than one person has thought I was drunk.

I have a hard time in sports stadiums with their steep stairs and narrow aisles, especially since the tickets are so expensive that we are always in the nose-bleed section, the cheap seats. Concerts and even weddings or showers try my patience. I get tired of sitting, and then I get tired of standing, and so it goes.

Anywhere there is a crowd, I can be knocked down easily, so I try to avoid them. I need an arm for support and comfort, yet even an impassioned embrace from a friend could set me spinning.

And, finally, there is driving—the one thing no one wants to give up. It's the thing we cling to as long as we can. It gives us freedom of movement and allows us not to be dependent on others for our needs.

At the time I write this, I can still drive, but I am not as comfortable as I once was. Not that I am a danger on the road. If I felt I was, believe me, I wouldn't be driving, at all. As long as I am aware of the route and don't have to locate somewhere new, I think I can handle it. Problem is, the more you don't do something, the worse it seems, and the harder it is to get back into it. I never really liked driving, anyway, and with one car in our driveway today, it is easier to let Hubby drive. To be honest, I am scared to get behind the wheel of a car, and that fear has fed upon itself until I have nearly talked myself out of driving ever again.

This means I am relying on Hubby for everything. How long can he deal with this? I know he would say forever, as I would to him if the situation were reversed. Yet, he has his life to live, too, and he can't spend it all waiting to catch me when inevitably I will fall. I realize that the independence I have felt in my home is eroding, which will probably force us to make decisions about our home and our lifestyle earlier than we wanted or expected. There are too many things to stumble over, both literally and physically, and too many stairs to climb. The Parkinson's has put us on the fast track to addressing major, life-changing decisions. Knowing that decisions made in haste may be regretted later, I worry. Life has become a balancing act. I know the limitations imposed by this disease, but I don't know when one of them will strike.

This chapter was supposed to be about birthdays. Birthdays are happy days, and I am getting too negative. I hope to celebrate many more birthdays in my home, wherever it might be, with grace and optimism and hope for the future.

ALL BY MYSELF

Last week could have been one of the worst weeks of my life, but it has been liberating, and I feel some of my old independence. You see, my husband went away for three days to an out-of-state meeting, which left me all alone in Florida to cope with who knew what might happen. While he was gone, I also had to drive guests to the airport and drive myself to an art class—and I hadn't been driving much. Both destinations were at least twenty miles away in heavy traffic that raced along, four lanes in each direction, and well over the speed limit. It was enough to make me want to pull the covers over my head and go back to bed. I faced the challenge with the help of my brother, and the day turned out better than I expected. He gave me directions while I did all the driving, and I got my confidence back!

Let me tell you—that was so very important to me. It was a great victory to learn that I could take care of myself for at least a short time. When we first began to spend our winters in Florida, I was amazed and pleased and surprised to see widows and other single women taking care of themselves alone. In their seventies, eighties, and some even in their nineties, they drove themselves to appointments, stores, and luncheons. Independent women. Like I used to be. Like I still want to be. And what better way to prove that I can still do this than to have Hubby travel out of state.

He was nervous, too. You know how you plan things, and while they seem like a good idea initially, when the time comes, you start thinking it wasn't such a great idea, after all? Hubby had those second thoughts about leaving me. I encouraged him to go. While I don't like being alone, at least I know I can still be the old me (as long as my baby brother is just a phone call away). I am sure Hubby probably liked having a break from me, also. I found it nice to sleep in the big bed all by myself, to watch whatever I wanted on TV, and to not be awakened when he rolls over with the covers several times a night.

I concluded that being away from a spouse and being by yourself is okay—as long as it doesn't happen too often.

MICHAEL J. FOX

I like to call Michael J. Fox my friend, but he is not really my friend-friend; he is my imaginary friend. When I am feeling bad about myself, I think of him and how he is still going after, what? Twenty years? I recently read about how he lives his life, and it is something I deeply embrace. When you have a disease like Parkinson's, it becomes part of you, part of your being. How can it not? You live with the uncertainty of what will happen next. You await the emergence of another symptom that will probably be worse than the ones you have. You want to know what to watch out for, but then again you don't really want to know. This disease also comes with the realization that, someday, your doctor is going to say, "I am sorry. There is not much more I can offer you." And you wonder what you will still be able to do when that day comes—or what won't you be able to do.

I think most people are surprised to hear that I am struggling with PD. I work at doing it gracefully. Still, no matter how hard I try to remain upbeat, there are moments when the reality of having PD hits me hard. I encounter situations that test my resolve, and I face the reality that someday the Parkinson's is going to win. I have friends who call me their hero, and some have said they are in awe of me. But, that's not me. After all, what choice do I have? I guess some people expect a person diagnosed with PD to hide in the house and stop embracing what life is left to them. But, that's not who I am. I was dealt a bad hand, and now I must play it for all it is worth.

Some days, it gets me down when my walk is not what you would call "normal." On those days, I feel old before my time, especially when someone asks if I need help. This seems to occur most often in the grocery store. For example, Hubby has to run back to the car or get a coupon or some such thing, while I stand there looking like an idiot amid the fruits and veggies or push my cart around and around, watching the door for his return. And he knows everybody in our small town and must greet everyone he sees and loves to talk. I think he could easily forget about the time and me. (I say I'm only kidding, but am I?) What is more, I cannot leave that spot, because when Hubby returns, I must be easy to find. (He must have grocery store issues to think that I could disappear into the store, never to be found again.) And often, as I am standing there, someone will ask me if I need help. When that happens, I wonder whether I really look as lost and alone as I feel, because I'm not that old. Then, I start to worry: Is this the Mask of Parkinson's?

On other days, I can hardly believe I have PD, and I move like nothing can hold me back.

While the disease is part of me and always present, I will not allow it to control my life or destroy the love and time I enjoy with my family and friends. Nor will it define who I am. It is something I will have to live with and adjust to as the need arises. Who knows, they may find a cure tomorrow. Sometimes I wonder why the researchers proceed so slowly, but keep on researching, guys. I know there will be a cure. Someday. Please try to make it in my lifetime.

THE BAD DAYS

When the bad times come, how do I deal with them? Luckily the really bad days have been few. Sometimes, though, everything just gets overwhelming. The bad days are not necessarily related to new physical limitations; most are emotional. I dwell on the negatives in my life and just want to sit and cry all day. I have to release the anger or sorrow that has accumulated. I've seen people on the news who have suffered unimaginable accidents: the loss of an arm or leg, being blinded, or worse. And, somehow, they managed to prevail and come through, not only with a new arm or leg or attitude, but also smiling. Somehow, they came to terms with their new limitations and found something to live for. In reading books by Michael J. Fox or books about the late Pope John Paul II and others who have experienced a life-changing diagnosis or event, I discovered that these individuals are not made of something the rest of us don't have. They shed many tears before achieving their personal goals.

None of us knows how we would react to a major upheaval until we are faced with one. Would we give up without a fight? Would we scour the internet for answers? Would we pray? Would we seek out more drug trials or more alternative medicines?

Would we shed a million tears? When I think about the many days and years ahead, I wonder if I will be able to handle them. I wonder whether I am strong enough to carry this burden for the rest of my life, whether I am strong enough to get on with my life. I believe I am. I hope I am, because I have many things to live for. I have a husband and son who need me. After all, Hubby still doesn't know where the pots and pans are after forty years in the same house!

Sadly, some choose to take a different way out. It is ironic that Robin Williams, whose gift of laughter comforted more people than he will ever realize, was hurting so badly on the inside. I wish he could have made himself laugh. I wish he had realized that someone or something would be there for him, to give him something to live for. I am sure that many things were hurting him, and no doubt the diagnosis of PD on top of it all was more than he could bear.

Sometimes, it takes a while to find something to live for. For example, I can only imagine how horrible it would be to wake up from an accident or illness and be told that you cannot function as the person you were. I am remembering Christopher Reeves, who was thrown from his horse and became a quadriplegic. He lost control of his entire body and was destined to live out the rest of his days confined to a wheel chair with a machine controlling every breath. Right after his accident, he said he wished he had died rather than have to face what he was facing. That was a natural, immediate reaction to what must have seemed an almost insurmountable challenge. Yet, he found that people were there to help, people who loved him unconditionally. He found something to live for.

This is why I continue to fight and don't let those I love see too much of my struggles. I have too much to live for: my family, my friends, myself. I was too young when I got this disease, and I am willing to fight to get back the time that I have lost, to recoup what PD has taken from me. Those of us burdened with this affliction have a large group fighting for us, fighting to find an answer and a cure—from our families to our doctors to the researchers. Maybe if we can hold on for a little longer, we will be equipped to handle this better than we thought we could. These are the reasons I am not giving up. I continue to fight. I continue to pray for a miracle.

Everyone has bad days, not just people with terrible diagnoses, and we all have our own ways of dealing with them, whether it's breaking something, having a crying fit, or running around the block. I have learned what is most important in life, and it is not my things; what's important are the people I love and cherish. As difficult as it may be for me and others to cope with Parkinson's, imagine what it is like for those who love us and who want to help us. Some of them would trade positions with us if they could, but they can't. They can't do anything to give us back what we have lost.

So, how do I deal with the not-so-perfect days? Sometimes for me, getting weepy or angry is a natural part of the bad days. None of us with PD knows the path the disease will take. I worry. Will it rob me of my mental capabilities as well as my physical ones? Will I exist in a nursing home until I am ninety, depleting all the money Hubby and I have saved to carry us through our golden years and still leave some for our son? Sometimes, when I am feeling overwhelmed—which isn't always just about

Parkinson's—I go into the bathroom, turn on the shower full-blast, and cry my eyes out. The warm water coupled with the Niagara Falls of tears makes me feel better. I come out, put on some sweet-smelling stuff, climb into my jammies, and have a chocolate chip cookie. It is how I ease the pain in my life so that I can cope. (To that end, I keep a batch of unbaked cookie dough rolled into little balls in my freezer so I can bake as many as I want whenever I want.) I guess the barometer of how I am feeling is the number of chocolate chip cookies in the freezer.

Telling the Kids

Cancer. MS. Alzheimer's. Parkinson's. ALS. Scary words to an adult. Scarier to a child or young person, especially when one is used to describe a parent. What do you do when you have to tell your children about your serious illness? Parents are supposed to always be there for their children, to protect them and take care of them. No matter how old you are, you seek out their help and support. They are the people you call to say your plane has landed safely or you got a promotion or just to talk about the weather.

And then, one day, you find out that you may not be around for your children for as long as you thought. Because Parkinson's is usually diagnosed late in life, most children who receive this news are adults, and this is not such a big issue. My son was thirteen when I received the diagnosis of Parkinson's, rather young to be told all the details of PD. My initial reaction was not to tell him about my condition until I had to. And being a teenaged boy, well, he was mostly interested in eating as much food as I could carry into the house and playing video games.

Of course, the age of the child as well as his or her personality and awareness are key here. Not telling your child you have a serious disease is not the answer. I knew I had to tell him. It nagged at me. I guess we all have a second nature when it comes to what's going on in a family, and kids are no different. There is that gut feeling that something is happening that they have no control over.

It was my son's doctor who convinced me to tell him. He reinforced my intuition that my son probably knew something was wrong and would be relieved to hear me talk about it openly. Of course, he was right. "Most important," he said, "your child needs to hear that you are dealing with something and that everything will be okay."

One day, I casually asked him if any of his friends had questioned why I was having trouble walking or getting up from a chair. Nope. No questions. I told him that I had Parkinson's, and while it was something discouraging and would probably slow me down, it wouldn't stop me. I said that if he had any questions, he should ask. He didn't blink. Back to the game.

I didn't pursue the matter further, but years later, I found out that he had confided in some of his friends. Did he turn to them for understanding and comfort instead of turning to me? Well, that was okay, I decided. At least I knew he was able to talk about it with someone

I rarely brought it up again. Good or bad thing to do? I don't know. Maybe I should have handled it differently, but I didn't want him to be worrying at a time in his life when, as a teenager facing his future after high school, he had enough of his own issues.

Grown up now, my son seems happy and well adjusted. What more could I want? As his doctor said, he probably knew that something was wrong even if he didn't understand the full consequences of the disease. Additionally, what if I had said nothing and he heard it from other kids? Would they even get the story correct? You know how teenaged boys are. Music is always blasting in their ears while their eyes are glued to some car chase game on their device. What's the chance he would hear everything a friend said correctly? Slim to none, would be my guess.

I now firmly believe that telling your children is best for everyone. Bringing problems into the open and encouraging dialogue is the best thing to do. And here's hoping I will be here for him for a long time. I am planning on it.

FIFTIES' FRIENDS/
THE GOLDEN YEARS

(Dedicated to my special friend, Connie G)

Many people move into and out of our lives. Some stay forever and become our closest friends. Others stay around because they are facing similar challenges at the same point in their lives. When my son was little, I hung out with his friends' moms. These were the sports moms, the music moms, the art moms, etc. You meet, develop a kinship, and when your worlds change for whatever reason, you all go your separate ways, hopefully as better people for having known each other. These are the people you run into in the grocery store. You say hi, exchange information, and promise to get together, but you both know it will not happen. It's not that you don't like each other or don't want to be friends; it's just that you both have moved on. That is why, when you find a true friend, you hold on to that person forever. When you say, "Remember when…" a true friend can finish your thoughts.

I visited a true friend, recently. We worked together many years ago. Over time, our circumstances changed and we lead separate lives, but we always keep in touch. We have shared many memories, some good, some not so much. She came to my wedding. I went to her husband's funeral. We were rooting for her when, as the married mom of four kids, she received her high school diploma after attending classes at night. I think she did it as much for her kids as for herself, to show them how hard it is to take care of a family and go to school at the same time. Probably our most special shared memory, and one that comes up every time we visit, is the day my son was baptized. As she held him, he fell asleep on her shoulder: She sat and rocked him for almost three hours. Couldn't even be dissuaded by the tray of lasagna in the kitchen. It is a story we both love to tell. No, it is not front-page news. It is just a special, sweet memory we share. And if there is someone new who hasn't heard the story, we tell it again in more detail.

Unfortunately, we now share something else. We share a neurological condition. My friend was diagnosed with ALS. I have Parkinson's. Two tough ones. During our visit, I discovered that we share the same feelings and frustrations and fears. We are both scared of what lies ahead, yet neither of us will look too deeply into that crystal ball because we don't really want to know all the details. Like me, she didn't tell people early on about her ALS because she didn't want them to worry. We both hold out hope for our conditions; when we see people who have had our disease longer and are doing well, it intensifies our hope that we can hold on longer. And if we see someone who was diagnosed at about the same time as we were and are not doing as well, we assume we can fight it better than the average person. Do you get it? We create a win-win situation.

With your true friends, you can be honest and open. You can share your fears and tears. You can say, "I know how you feel," and mean it, or just say nothing at all. True friends are simply there for each other in the good times and the bad, praying for each other and believing that everything will be okay. Because it will be. And so it goes.

I Peeked

Once I took that first glance into my crystal ball and saw that Parkinson's would severely challenge me, I thought I would never look into it again. I didn't need to see in black and white what it would do to my life. I ignored all the articles written about PD, all the articles promising new treatments that seemed too complex to understand, and all the articles written by people who, shall we say, hope to make money from those of us longing for a cure

Eventually, though, I took another peek. What made me look again? It was my (imaginary) friend, Michael J. Fox. I saw a blurb on TV that he was planning to star in a new comedy series, and I thought, "Wow! That is quite an undertaking and commitment. Maybe he has discovered something that will help us all. Has his research found something new?"

When you have any condition that does not yet have a "cure," you will jump at anything that seems to promise relief. So, I took a deep breath and peered into my crystal ball again. In my second look, I read that a different schedule of medication had helped Michael control the tics that are so obvious with PD. It was nothing earth-shattering, but it renewed my hope that we are getting closer to a cure. Maybe it will be as simple as reevaluating the meds we are presently taking. I have always said that my best medicine was not found in a bottle, but in the hope I held out for a cure. Maybe Michael's experience has heralded the next step.

Although I avoided the literature, over the years, I attended several presentations about Parkinson's. I know we all walk into the room hoping to hear about some remarkable new discovery that will return us to wholeness. I understand that they want to get it right, but the researchers seem to be moving at a snail's pace. It is so hard to hear that nothing new has happened in the march to a cure. Even so, after learning about Michael's new show and realizing he was undertaking a major challenge for someone with PD, I felt good all day. It renewed my hope that a cure is still being sought. When I meet Michael, I must thank him for his determination and stamina and his ability to give me a renewed dose of hope in fighting the horrors of PD. He gives me the strength to hold on. He makes me feel that a cure will be found shortly—and you can be sure I will bring out the chocolate chip cookies to celebrate.

PILLS ARE ME

Today, it occurred to me that my life has become like that game Whack A Gopher, in which you bop the gophers as they stick their gopher heads out of their gopher holes, and of course, they keep popping out faster and faster. The gophers represent the symptoms of my PD. Each time another nasty manifestation of the disease rears its ugly head, my doc gives me a new med or changes how much I take, and that nasty thing goes away. So far, so good; but as the meds become less effective, I will be left with a whole bunch of gophers and nothing to bop them with.

Can you imagine what is happening in my brain that I am comparing my life to an arcade game?

I am sick of taking all these pills that keep me going. I have orange ones, yellow ones, and the ubiquitous white ones. They come in rounds and ovals, and some are encapsulated and boast two colors. As much as I hate them, if I don't take them, I will be even sicker. What a problem. I have lost count of the number of pills I take a day. All I know is that my day is structured around my pill-taking schedule. I have to carry a bottle of water or something to drink at all times in case I am out and have no easy access to liquid. Ever try to dry-swallow a pill? No way. I took a large pill with an ice cream cone, once, and it was a lot harder than you would think.

When I was little, I couldn't swallow pills. My mom crushed up orange baby aspirin tablets between two spoons and added a little water to get them into me. I still remember that taste. Yuck. Now, though, I have learned to swallow pills standing up, sitting down, at a water fountain, or with a glass of water, and I can take up to six at a time. Taking so many pills is a pain in the butt—and it is a constant reminder that Parkinson's rules my life. Like I need another reminder.

I am an expert at pill-swallowing, or so I thought until an incident in the drugstore parking lot. I was sitting in the car, waiting for Hubby (so what else is new), and it was pill-popping time. I tossed a bunch in my mouth, followed by a big swig of water…and I started to choke. Hubby arrived, pulled me out of the car, and tried to do the Heimlich maneuver, something he is not familiar with, until some kind gentleman arrived and did it successfully. The man disappeared before I could thank him. The incident scared the hell out of Hubby and the bystanders in the parking lot. For me, it was embarrassing and eye-opening. It's odd, but I was not really frightened, maybe because I could still wheeze and could feel my breath returning as the pills melted. However, the incident alarmed me enough that I am now less cavalier about pill-popping. I take fewer pills at a time and more slowly. Still, after it had occurred three times, we both decided to take CPR classes.

Now, as I used to do for my aunts and mother once a week, once a week I sit down with my own little green boxes that are labeled with the days of the week and the time of day. I count out my pills and dole them out, six yellow ones in the daytime slots, round white ones in the night slots, and so on. This is easier and faster than doing it once a day, and I highly recommend it. Taking pills becomes so mechanical that I could easily question whether I have, in fact, taken them. And I haven't gotten to the point where I mix them up, God forbid. When I refreshed my aunt's stash, I often found today's pills already taken and tomorrow's half gone, and we won't even discuss Fridays, so I know what can happen. Fortunately, the little boxes let me know whether I have taken a particular med. I hope there are no more additions to my pill-popping, because I am running out of boxes.

THE UGLIEST WORDS IN THE ENGLISH LANGUAGE

I once saw a survey in which English professors were asked what they thought was the most beautiful word in the English language. They chose lullaby, a truly smooth and lovely word. I kinda like lollipop, and beautiful is a beautiful word in itself. Lately, however, I have had to use some of the ugliest words in the English language. I have learned the meaning of words that no one wants to add to their vocabulary. Words that spell-check can't even find. Some that Dr. Rathi brandishes around to tell me what is going on in my brain include:

Dystonia: A brain disorder that affects the muscles

Dopamine antagonists

Carbidopa levadophe: What I take to make me feel better

Dyskinesia: A category of movement disorder relating to involuntary movements

Dopamine: A hormone and neurotransmitter that makes me feel better

Oh, give me back the beautiful words I discovered first!

In addition to the words above—and others like them—I have been using two words that are even more ugly: I can't. I am saying these words more often because the PD is starting to grate on my nerves in minor, but annoying ways. When I sleep, I sleep well and soundly for a few hours, but then I wake up early. When I retired, I expected that I would sleep until at least eight-thirty. For me, back then, that would have been a little piece of heaven. Now, I am up before seven, having gone to bed around midnight. I don't feel as tired as you might think, but every so often I get exhausted and need a nap right smack dab in the middle of the day when there is so much going on. The meds are failing me earlier and earlier in the day, and of course, that adds to the exhaustion. All these annoying little things tell me that I haven't stopped this demon, yet.

Once the meds lose their power…what happens then? Already I don't like to attend large functions because I am somewhat unsteady on my feet. I feel out of place and my body stiffens. Oh, and this is something new: there is a little dance I do when I am just trying to stand around. It causes me to swing and sway like someone rocking a baby or someone who is singing and really getting into the music. Even when I concentrate on it, I can't stop it. The more I try to stop it, the more I swing and sway. This symptom becomes more pronounced when I am in a hurry or angry or annoyed about something.

I used to believe that I could do anything as long as I had instructions and the proper tools or direction. Not so much, anymore. For my body to give me trouble, to do what it wants to do and not what I want it to do—is unconscionable. I don't like it one bit.

This PD thing has dogged me for ten years. Ten years has always been the benchmark date for how long the meds generally work, and this is the first time I can see any changes. Frankly, they scare the heart out of me. I had hoped I could fight this thing, and I am not giving up, but a nagging little voice in the back of my head is turning into a bigger voice telling me, "You can't control this." It keeps getting louder.

When the meds lose their effectiveness, I feel it immediately. I feel like a switch has been shut off and will not turn on again until I pop another pill (or four or five). My legs get heavy. I shuffle around the house. Sometimes, my body just wants to sit down in a comfy chair and not move until my strength comes back.

I have read that the best way to manage the meds is to keep them level and steady throughout the day, which is exactly the opposite of what I had been doing. Now, I am trying to adjust my pill-taking to cover the time when I have the most to do without completely upsetting my medicinal routine. I am giving that a shot.

BOTOX AND MEDICAL MARIJUANA

Besides the pills I take, there are other treatments for Parkinson's—Botox and medical marijuana.

The jury is still out on Botox and its application to Parkinson's. I have been receiving Botox shots in my neck because it was getting quite stiff and making it hard to turn my head, which is more than a little matter when it comes to driving and checking the passing lane. (I know I don't drive much, but this new symptom is making it impossible.) Dr. Rathi told me the shots would help by relaxing the muscles in my neck. I was having trouble sleeping because of the pain, so I decided to try it.

Now this is the thing about Botox: the last syllable of Botox is tox as in toxin, as in poison. Why in the world am I putting yet another poison in my body? Twenty-plus shots, four times a year. The shots don't hurt; they just sting a little, and they do work. I feel much better. After a while, though, I questioned the need to continue. Was I feeling all that much better? Was this an outcome achievable through exercise, massage therapy, or another means? I would have to stop the injections to find that answer. So, I told Dr. Rathi that I didn't want to take them anymore. He questioned my concerns (and probably my intelligence) and said I would just become stiffer. In the interest of taking control over my own treatment, I stopped the treatment for about four months. In time, I noticed my neck was hurting again, so I went back to the Botox. Still worried about my neck muscles, I asked Dr. Rathi to give me a lesser amount of the drug, and that is working just as well, but it only lasts for three or four months.

Around the same time, we started attending meetings of support groups in the area. At the first meeting of the breakout session, when the caregivers met, they discussed Botox. Since I had been on it for several years, Hubby wondered if the drug was living up to expectations or if I could get as much relief from a neck pillow or other forms of therapy. To a person, the caregivers all voiced their strong disapproval of the drug. I did my own investigation, which revealed that sometimes the drug migrates to a place it is not supposed to be. After my last round of shots, I couldn't pick my head up without it falling backwards again; it felt like it weighed fifty pounds. (Must be all that brain matter!) To be serious, though, it felt almost as if I had gotten too much relaxant in some areas so that the muscles didn't respond when I called on them to lift my head. It was a terrible feeling. I hope it is due to the Botox and not to the spread of the disease.

The thing is, the Botox works. My neck feels much better. I can look over my shoulder with no pain. I will continue to monitor this drug closely.

And then, if the shots don't work there is…medical marijuana.

What a country. Connecticut recently approved medical marijuana for use in managing some diseases, like Parkinson's. It will be a while before all the specifics are worked out, but it poses some interesting possibilities. Of course, I want to see if it will help in the battle with a challenging disease like PD, but I admit that it will be interesting to discover what I missed out on the first time around. I was a child of the Sixties, a good girl, one of those Catholic high school girls. I never tried marijuana; I never used any recreational drugs. I wondered how anyone could put something in their body that could cause them to lose control of themselves. Also, I was rarely in a situation where it was available. Thank goodness. Things might have been different, but I think not. I didn't drink, either. Boring. How did anybody think I was any fun? (Luckily, my husband did. He was one of those good Catholic high school boys.)

I am hopeful that marijuana will make some of the annoying symptoms of Parkinson's go away and help with the many diseases for which we have no long-term answers. My neurologist is firmly in favor of its use for medical reasons. He recommends it for calming the queasy stomach often brought about by my heavy-duty drugs. I don't know if it will be helpful to me since my body has adjusted to the drugs that made me violently ill in the beginning. At the very least, it will be another drug to turn to when all else fails.

Now, here is something amusing to contemplate: Until the state approves the production and distribution channels, we have to find it on our own! Can you imagine me prowling the streets looking for some weed? If I have a card from my doc, I can buy it—without being arrested. I am keeping an eye on this situation. Maybe I won't be boring anymore!

Since I wrote the above, Connecticut gave approval to six facilities in the state where, with a doctor's approval, the drug will be dispensed. I don't know the effect this will have on PD patients. I guess more studies have to be done. Dr. Rathi asked me if I wanted a script for it, but since he sees its primary benefit to be control of nausea caused by the meds and I no longer have that problem, I will wait to see if other uses of marijuana are discovered for PD patients. I was kind of hoping that it could be used for other symptoms, like walking or freezing. If I could just return to my old self and have the physical energy to keep up with my mind, it would be wonderful.

My Bucket List

I guess we all have a bucket list, whether we formalize it or not. These are generally the things we want to do or see before we are too old to do and see them. I imagine the majority of items for most people would be about visiting a place we have always dreamed of or accomplishing an academic, professional, or personal goal.

My bucket list includes things that are not easily accomplished, things just out of my reach, things I have to strive for, work a little harder for. Some of them, I may accomplish. Others will require hard work. And some I probably will never be able to cross off the list. Yet, I know that often the journey and the discoveries along the way can be more sweet and fulfilling than the actual outcome. Undoubtedly, my bucket list will change from year to year as I accomplish my dreams or forego some for other pursuits.

My first desire was to get a tattoo. Done. Been there, done that. Love it, love it, and love it! I suspect some of my friends think I am nuts. Some people don't understand why I would do such a thing to my body. And, of course, the older a person is, the more he or she is inclined not to like it. I can hear the Golden Girls now, saying in one voice: "Why would you do this to your body?" But, I love it. Did I say that already? It is a dragonfly on a flower, turquoise and pink and green. It's on my right shoulder.

Believe me when I say it is not your father's tattoo. It has a special meaning to me. When my father died, a friend gave me a beautiful garden stepping-stone along with a story entitled, "The Parable of the Dragonfly." In many cultures, the dragonfly is a symbol of everlasting life, meaning we will all meet again in a better place than this one. Maybe I see it as staying young a little longer. Or maybe I am just a rebel, living on the edge. Yes, that's funny, I know. I have been told that I am the last person anyone thought would get a tattoo. That says a lot about the kind of person people think I am. I probably did it because I like to keep them guessing. And who better to sport a tattoo than an artist who loves color? It can be hidden under my sleeve, but I plan to show it off as much as possible.

One older gentleman we met on vacation was frankly taken aback at the tattoo and didn't hesitate to make his negative feelings known. While I liked and admired the man and respected his opinion, it didn't matter one bit to me what he thought about my tattoo. He seemed to see it as a defilement of my body, but I love it. Later, he told me he had given the issue some thought and apologized. He said it was my business what I did with my body, and he felt sorry that I might have found him too critical. Maybe actually seeing the tattoo and how colorful and pretty it was, that it wasn't a dark skull and crossbones, mellowed him.

I have been seriously thinking of getting another one on my leg. I have already designed it. It will be a bass guitar, the body of which is shaped like an artist's palette, and its stem like paintbrushes.

The next item on my bucket list was to be a published author, to see my name on a real book. It would fulfill a lifelong dream, one that began in kindergarten and continues to this day. I would be interviewed on all the talk shows and have it read by millions of people. I would have book signings. Well, why not? If I am going to dream, I am going to dream big! And if you are reading my words, now, then I have accomplished that goal. I started with a blog, and it has turned into a wonderful and amazing book that I actually wrote. It truly is a labor of love that so far has taken me over two years to write and edit. I had thought I would just compile my blog posts into book form and away I would go. Not so fast. It required renewed soul-searching and rewriting and rewriting until I couldn't look at it anymore. I hope it will make someone with PD laugh or cry or even give someone the strength to hang on until a cure comes our way.

I would like to sell my paintings for lots of money—and not to people I know. I would like to be represented by a gallery somewhere along the coast of Maine who will take my work and display it on their walls, and actually sell it. I am happiest when the brush is in my hand and colors are mixed on my palette. I can forget about the PD as I try to capture the beauty around me. Even if a painting is not coming out well, the serenity and satisfaction and calmness I feel as I paint outshines all the money anyone could give me. This is the part I want the most, the doing of it, but I will take the gallery dream if it is presented to me.

I also want to learn how to play Pachelbels Canon on the piano. I have my father's piano and the music; what I don't have is his talent. I try to play the music, though. It helps limber up my fingers, stiff from Parkinson's. It keeps my mind in gear as I try to remember how to read music. My daddy is still watching out for me.

I also want to learn how to use Facebook more skillfully. God only knows what I may have posted due to my ignorance.

Currently, the last item on my bucket list is to meet my imaginary friend, Michael J. Fox. I would give him a kiss and a hug and tell him to keep up the good work he does. He probably doesn't know how many people he helps, and I would like to tell him so. I will bring the chocolate chip cookies.

No doubt, I will add to, revise, and tweak this list. I may not accomplish all of these items. But, who cares? I might. And what I learn along the way will be awesome.

THE FALL

Well, it was bound to happen. One of the first things a doctor asks a Parkinson's patient is, "Have you had any falls?" I used to feel oh-so smug when I answered, "No." Last week, that changed. Maybe it wasn't the PD that made me fall. Maybe it was just the ground. Yet, I can hear Dr. Rathi say, just as smug as I had been, "Well, have you ever fallen before?" The answer was No.

So, there it is. I have crossed over to the dark side, the side where I have to admit I may not be as steady on my feet as I would like. However first, let me explain what happened. Hubby and I decided to go for a walk. It was very hot, I was tired, and we were walking rather briskly. Because I was tired, I probably wasn't picking up my feet as I should. We came to a kind of transition from a concrete sidewalk to a wooden boardwalk, and my toe must have caught on something. I did not feel anything catch, or I might have been able to steady myself. Instead, I took a faceplant onto the walkway.

Let me tell you, no one was more surprised than I was. As I was going down, slow motion kicked in, and I remembered seeing my mom take a fall on some concrete steps and emerge bloody. I was becoming my mom! My hubby was right next to me, petrified that something major had happened. I could tell by his voice that he was quite upset but, as is my nature, I brushed it off. If I accepted that the fall had occurred as a consequence of the PD, I wouldn't be okay. I would be acknowledging my limitations. So, it was just the change in the terrain, not the PD, I concluded. I got up rapidly, grateful that no one had seen me fall. I assessed the damages. Nothing felt broken, but my face was scratched and raw. We walked back to the house, where I realized my hand was throbbing. After a quick visit to one of the walk-in clinics, I learned that I had sprained my hand badly and had a black eye. Good conversation starter.

I mended physically from the effects of the fall, but mentally, I took a big hit: I cannot be and do what I used to be and do. That is a difficult thing to admit. I feel vulnerable and uncertain. I know I am not alone. Even without PD, this is what we all face as we age.

And guess what? Hubby just rolled out of bed, and the first thing he asked me was, "Want to go for a walk?"

Are you kidding me? Of course, I will go for a walk, but this time I'll take my walking stick.

A BALANCING ACT: MY TRICYCLE

When you have Parkinson's or a myriad other neurological conditions, there are certain things you cannot do. Most are related to balance, and nowhere does that become more evident than when trying to ride a bike. You know that expression: "It's like riding a bike. Once you know how to do it, you never forget." Well, I certainly haven't forgotten, but I physically can't do it anymore. It disappointed me. I love the freedom a bike brings. You see more than when you ride in a car. You are outside in the fresh air, getting exercise. Yes, you're also outside when you walk, but you can cover more territory on a bike. As I have said, Hubby helps me when I venture outside and into crowds, but I don't want my world to close in on me. I want to continue to live life, just at my own pace.

I tried to continue with the bicycle, but…I fell off. Sort of. I can't lift my feet to balance me when I stop—you know, those short hops you take to steady yourself. I just cannot do that anymore. So, my sweet husband, bless his heart, dragged me (not quite kicking and screaming) into a bicycle store, and I came out with a tricycle, of all things. It is really cute. I had been reading about the effectiveness of bicycle therapy for PD patients. In both riding a bike and using a treadmill, the repetitive act of moving your feet and legs becomes second-nature again and helps you to walk naturally.

The tricycle is blue, like my eyes, and it has a basket on the back between the large wheels where I can carry food for a picnic or a small dog, and it is surprisingly difficult to ride—or maybe the word is different—but I got used to it. The tricycle is very stable, but also quite sensitive to a slight turn. When we ride, I go first and Hubby follows. The road we take has sewers along the side, and he is constantly screaming, "Stay out of the gutters. You'll fall and get hurt!" Well, doesn't he think I know that? Like I'm gonna do it on purpose! I will probably fall because he is screaming at me. After riding a bicycle for years, it takes a bit of time to adjust to a new system. I'd like to let him try it and see if he doesn't revert to old habits.

And so it goes. I tool around town with my three wheels and basket. Everyone who sees me stops to comment on the contraption. I think everyone wants one, now.

I have graduated to a "senior" bike, a three-wheeler. Is it an old people's bike? Of course not. It is a great form of transportation, much steadier than a two-wheeler, big-girl bike, but I love it. Maybe I have finally stopped caring about what I look like. I'm just having fun and trying to stay healthy.

CANDY CANES

I have decided to use a cane in selected situations. Not because I really need it, but because it will make it easier for me to get around. I won't use it everywhere, just in crowded places or when I will be walking for a long time. One reason for my decision is the fall I took recently; it scared me. The Parkinson's has caused me to lose my balance. I walk sideways, which is a good way to describe why I am all over the sidewalk, as Michael J. Fox described it in an AARP article. If you have experienced this, you will understand. When you are in a crowded place, even just on a crowded walkway, if you look around at the sights while moving or look down to find something in your pocketbook, you may lose your balance and suddenly discover that you are walking not in a straight line, but sideways. I am sure many people think I'm drunk.

I have one concern about using a cane: Am I giving in to the disease? I fear it is an acknowledgement of my frailties. Is the disease progressing? Does the cane symbolize the beginning of the fall into the dark quiet of PD? The answer is yes. A little voice in the back of my head is telling me I have beaten this for eleven years already and how much time do I want?

I want a lot more. And why do I think I can beat this when no one else can? Because I have to believe it. I'm sure my use of a cane will bring many more glances and questions from people who don't know me well, but see me when I'm shopping or in church. No doubt, I will be asked if I sprained an ankle or broke my foot. At this point, I will tell them what ails me. Maybe, somehow, that will inspire someone to work harder at finding a cure.

I must pick a cane. If you think I am planning to walk around with a plain wooden or metal cane, then you don't know me. It has to be unique and colorful and way out there. I imagine a candy cane and laugh. Fortunately, an artist friend gave me a beautiful, decoupage cane. It will be my first cane. I imagine there is a cadence to walking with a cane, and I will have to find that. In the meantime, watch out world. Here I come, and I am armed.

I know, I'm the person who hates being stared at, and yet got a colorful tattoo on her shoulder and is now venturing into the world with a flourish and an eye-popping cane. It doesn't seem to make sense, but there you go.

You may be interested in what I have observed while using a cane. Sometimes I feel like Moses coming down from wherever he came down from and, when he merely raised his staff, the waters parted. I admit I can't part the waters, but people certainly do step aside and let me pass. When we were in Paris this spring, whenever I was in line and had my cane, someone invariably tapped me on the shoulder and directed me to another, faster line so I didn't have to stand and wait. I must say that I feel bad when a woman older than me offers her seat. I don't want to take it, but I end up sitting, and she ends up standing. It is hard to say no to an older woman.

I notice that I am using the cane more often. It steadies me and hopefully will prevent me from falling into that glass case, as I am so afraid of doing.

Long Boating

We just came back from a most wonderful trip. For my sixtieth birthday, we took a longboat through Central Europe, stopping in Budapest, Slovakia, Austria, and Germany, and ending up in Amsterdam. We both love to travel and figured this was the easiest way to go, unpacking once and then gliding slowly through the river mists and the most beautiful countries I have ever seen.

Having Parkinson's is always a challenge because you don't know what you can and can't do until you try. The problem is, you may fall on your butt trying and get hurt badly. I am pleased to report that I could do just about everything on our trip—except dance. But then, I wasn't so good at that before the PD.

When Hubby first proposed the trip, I was hesitant. Fifteen days on a ship sounded like a long time. Would I get seasick? Would I go stir crazy living in one room for two weeks? Would I be able to keep up with the tour group? Happily, I discovered that the tours off-ship were geared for three different levels of difficulty, and I was able to keep up with everything—except for uneven paths to a dark castle at one stop and another stop where I climbed halfway up the stairs inside a windmill before I figured out that any higher and you might as well teach me to be a wind master, because I wasn't going to be able to get down.

I had no difficulty with the walking tours of the major cities along the rivers. The paths and sidewalks were cobblestone and uneven, but I had my trusty cane to keep me from tripping. As I mentioned earlier, large groups of people blocking sidewalks and doorways parted when they witnessed the lady with the cane.

I must admit, I kinda liked it until I realized the people who were offering me their seats on a bus or other kindnesses were older than I and deserved and probably needed this courtesy more than I did. But they were very insistent that I take their offer so I did. Before I started using my cane, I was the one offering help. What could I do but graciously accept? This was a new learning experience. It taught me to be grateful for all the caring people in this world and it showed me what it will be like to be on the receiving end for help. And it showed me that my cane speaks a universal language.

I worry that the disease will progress to the point where I can't handle the rigors of traveling, anymore. Traveling is not easy. Lines are long; plane seats are cramped. You must sign up early for your choice of destination, and when you have PD, anything can happen between the time you sign on and the time you depart. Hubby reminds me, though, that anything can happen to anyone at any time.

MIRROR, MIRROR

My mirror is broken. And I don't mean that it's smashed into a million pieces. I mean that it must be defective after all these years of use. When I look into it, I think I see my mother looking back. Come to think of it, all the mirrors must be broken, because the person I see reflected is certainly not the person I see in my mind.

Appearances. This is a tough subject to write about because it is so personal and shows how vain I am. There is only one way to say this without embarrassing myself and sounding conceited and that is to just address it outright: PD does a job on your appearance. What happens when someone who has lived her life being told she is pretty is not so pretty anymore? How does a person who has always been complimented on her looks accept that she is no longer young and looking good? How do you face a disease that steals that youthfulness prematurely?

I always claimed that physical appearance was not important to me. Unfortunately, it is. Each day when I look in that mirror, I see new wrinkles looking back. This person I see looks like me, but she is old and wrinkled and tired looking. Not at all like the person who is looking at her.

At best I look fifty; at worst, I look fifty, or so I would like to believe. Where did this person come from? Lights can bring out all your wrinkles, and Hubby recently changed all the bulbs. That must be it. These new lights show all your flaws. Now that I had an answer, I walked out of the bathroom into a more complimentary light with a fifty-year-old smile on my sixty-one-year-old face, leaving that old lady behind.

No matter what our mirrors tell us, I believe most of us leave that person in the bathroom mirror home when we turn to face the world. An art professor once told me that if we were to draw a self-portrait without looking in a mirror or at a photograph, we would draw ourselves as more attractive than we are. We do not see ourselves as we are. For most of my life, I was told I was pretty, and I believed it. Now, I have to deal with the transition from "a pretty lady" to "she must have been pretty when she was younger." The woman in the mirror is yet another injustice that can be blamed on Parkinson's.

PD changes your appearance in many ways. It does a job on your posture, on how you walk, on how you smile. I can't wear those sexy high heels. I am sure I would look fabulous—and would probably break a leg the minute I stood up on them. Yeah, very sexy. And no more tight shirts; they just call attention to my round shoulders and horrible posture. Eventually my face and smile will freeze. Oh, I should have seen it coming! When my mom was in a nursing home, the staff frequently commented on how much I looked like my mother. My mom was ninety-three, then. I am sure I don't look anywhere near ninety-three. She looked like me, not the other way around.

I would be the first to say that what a person looks like has no bearing on what kind of person he or she is. I have noticed that the most attractive people are not necessarily those I am drawn to. A person becomes beautiful when you look in their eyes and see their soul. Nevertheless, it is a hard reality to accept that you are not the person you remember, the one who could turn heads.

I trace my feelings about my appearance to my early years. I had three moms—my mom and her two unmarried sisters. These are the ones I call the Golden Girls. The aunts lived right next door—and I was the only niece. Now, these aunties were very conscious of physical appearances. Especially mine. When I was four or five, my aunts liked to take me to fancy restaurants. We dressed for these occasions, and I believe gloves were part of the ensemble. As we walked into the restaurant, my aunts were sure to point out, "Everybody is looking at you because you are so pretty." This china doll they were playing with was shy and self-conscious and didn't appreciate it one bit. It upset me; I didn't like people staring at me for any reason. Unfortunately, because of all that emphasis placed on my appearance, I am more vain than I like to admit. To this day, I can't walk into a room without feeling that all eyes are probing me. I try to slink in quickly and find a place to sit.

As my physical symptoms become more pronounced, this fear of facing people's stares may be my downfall. I can see wanting to remain hidden, and Parkinson's has been described as an illness in which people shut themselves off from others. I can understand that, and yet I know it is stupid thinking. I don't want to miss anything, but I don't want to be stared at for the wrong reasons. And where I can or can't go will depend upon my symptoms at the time. When my hand is unsteady, for example, you would not want to sit next to me in a restaurant. I might end up tossing food on you.

Surpassing vanity by far is the boost that looking my best can give me. Feeling I look good is vital to helping me feel good. When I put on a new outfit I have splurged on, I feel more confident. I can't help but strut a bit (if I can). A good appearance conveys power. Every day, no matter how I feel, I get out of bed and get dressed and remind myself to make every effort to make myself beautiful for my age and comfort level.

Concern about what people think of us is normal. We all want to be accepted. But, what a waste of time and effort! It has taken me forty years to realize that others' opinions do not matter. If I am satisfied with myself, that is good enough for me. How could anyone else know what I want from life? How can they know my fears and desires or what I want to do with my life? Except for a few people I admire, what others think of me is of no concern—most of the time. Or that is what I want to believe. It doesn't matter. I have also noticed that no matter how old I get, sometimes those stupid little fears rear their ugly heads. I want to fit in. I want to be accepted.

It takes a strong personality to live your own way and not how others want you to live. That is called maturity, and it is something a lot of people never get.

Eleven Years/Growing Older

The eleven-year mark has arrived, along with another birthday. I had no idea what I might be experiencing when I reached this point. I have to admit that I am doing better than I expected. Probably it has been possible for me to be largely in denial for all these years because PD has so far been more of a nuisance than a life-impacting issue. How much longer will I be able to say that?

Let's face it: there is no way to put a genuinely positive spin on getting old. Yes, some people grow old gracefully, so they say, but how many people do you know who have? I know one. Then there's that nonsense about embracing your wrinkles because each one has a meaning. I presume this suggests I want to remember the time I was awake all night because my son was out with a girl who gave me bad vibes, the wrinkle I have from rushing him to the ER when he broke his collarbone playing football, or the ones I got from worrying about him on tour with his band. Those are only a few of my wrinkles. And now, I am dragging along this PD thing with me everywhere, and it is a real wrinkle-producer.

Sorry. I am having a bad day. Yes, it's true that growing older is not for sissies. You lose people you love. I recently lost my mom, the last of that generation. I guess I am the matriarch, now. My aunts told me I would miss them when they were gone, and they were right. I do miss them. I miss the way we celebrated holidays, the special food only they knew how to make, the recipes they never wrote down, and the history of our small family. No matter how you try to duplicate the experiences of your childhood, you never can, because you learn that it is the people who made it special and not the stuff.

Now, the players have changed. So, like us all, I have moved on and created my own traditions. I hope my son will view them as being as loving and as special as I remember my traditions from childhood.

A Difficult Year

The year 2012 was horrible. I kept wishing that someone would push it off a cliff. Many of my friends lost their mothers, including me. Others lost brothers, fathers, and friends. Some have seen a cancer return with more vengeance, and some have grown tired of the fight. There have been shootings in my state of Connecticut, shootings that never should have happened and never would have happened if the good guys were the only ones carrying guns. Twenty babies died along with six adults, and I hope it does not take any more than that before we have some real movement on gun control. Why a person not involved with law enforcement or the military should be able to put their hands on an assault rifle is beyond my comprehension.

The biggest disappointment this year for me personally is that there are still no cures for many major, life-stealing diseases, like Parkinson's, MS, Alzheimer's, ALS, and cancer. At the time of my diagnosis, researchers expected a cure for Parkinson's in ten years. Well, ten years have passed, and I am still waiting. The meds I take remain viable for ten years, on average. Ten years is a long time to wait. Ten years ago, I believed a new drug would pop up any day and allow me to get on with my life. Well, it hasn't, and it is harder and harder to believe that one will.

Here's the thing: The day-to-day physical aspects of PD—stumbling, dropping things—take over your life. Even though I have tried mightily not to let them take over mine, they have. They take over even the simplest of things we all take for granted. PD is always there, the first thing I think of when I wake up, and the last thing I think about when I climb into bed. It has made me feel broken and unattractive and unable to do what I really want, when I want to do it. It has made me afraid of the future and where I will be when it arrives.

Now, everything I see I am looking at through shattered glasses, glasses shattered by my glimpse into that crystal ball more than eleven years and many more tears ago. The future is no longer mine to command and plan.

I Hope You Have a Nice Evening

From the minute I was told I had PD, I knew I was supposed to do something. I did not know what. I do believe everything happens for a reason. Bad things, too. All I can do is take what I have been handed and try to make it right. For example, when my husband and I were seriously injured by a drunk driver, we helped to establish Mothers Against Drunk Driving (MADD) in our community to save others from the same fate or worse.

Writing is also my therapy. It has forced me to figure out what is important in life and to live each day the best I can, making sure I make someone else feel good, even if all I can give is a smile.

Recently, when the Mass was over at church, the woman next to me turned and said, "I hope you have a very nice evening." I was surprised. We didn't know each other. Still, it was such a nice thing to say. Of course, I wished her the same. What a nice gesture that was! It makes me smile to think of it, and I try to remember to pay it forward. When someone acknowledges me or compliments me, I feel good all over, and it lasts the entire day. These small gestures that don't cost a thing can lift someone's spirits more than we will ever know.

Everyone has been given something special—a unique gift to brighten or inform the world and help others. It would be truly a sin not to use our gifts to make our little part of the world a little better for all of us. That woman's simple statement resonated with me, and I never forget it.

How I Start My Days

I hate getting up in the morning, getting ready, and getting dressed. It has become such a chore. My idea of an ideal day is to stay in my jammies all day. Don't do enough of that. My husband is just the opposite. His idea is to get errands done early in the day and have the rest of the time to do other stuff. He always complains that a noon or midday appointment ruins the whole day. But, this is our life together, and if we have a late morning appointment, then so be it. I have to honor my limits and my comfort factor when I plan my activities.

Lately, I am awake at four a.m. I lie in bed, my mind racing with things I have to do or want to do. What shall I write about, today? I get great ideas and then promptly forget them when I get up. I hate to get out of a warm, comfortable bed even to use the bathroom. My body takes a while to limber up and do what I ask of it: dressing, pill-popping, getting breakfast, all of which most others do without putting much effort into it. Some mornings, I'm afraid I will try to stand up and my legs won't support me for that quick run. On those mornings, I lie in bed until I am sure my arms and legs are still moving and up to the task. I hope I will have a clue when the next stage of PD rears its head. My experience so far tells me it will develop slowly, and I will be ready for it, but you never know.

To ease the matter of getting ready in the morning, I decide what to wear before I go to bed, especially if we have to leave very early. And if we have to get up really early to catch a plane, for example, I have been known to sleep in my underwear. Frankly, I would sleep in my clothes if they didn't wrinkle. It would be so wonderful to get out of bed already prepared for the day ahead!

You might be surprised at how many small things you can do to make your life easier, in the morning and all day. To ease the problem of having a hard time bending over, I have moved the items I use most in the kitchen to shelves I can reach easily. Pots and pans on the shelf where glasses go? Why not? Hubby used to laugh at my parents because they set the table for breakfast before they went to bed. I understand, now. I hate getting up and getting the bowl, spoon, milk, and cereal out. Do it the night before, and you are golden. My hubby doesn't laugh at me anymore. The way I see it, if it makes sense to you, and it works—do it.

WHAT PARKINSON'S DISEASE HAS TAUGHT ME

_It is okay to ask for help.

_Family and friends are more important than anyone or anything else.

_Occasionally, you have to laugh at yourself.

_We all need to watch more sunsets and sunrises. They are different every day.

_I am vainer than I thought.

_You must find a doctor you can trust and believe in.

_Be willing to question your doctor's judgment and seek your own answers when necessary.

_Ask your doctor to speak English, not medical English.

_It helps to have a doctor who can laugh and who makes time for you when you need it.

_It is okay to cry, but for every ten minutes you cry, you must laugh for twenty.

_Exercise is important.

_Exercise is important. (This is not a typo.)

_Religion, prayer, and meditation are comforting.

_What works for someone else may not work for you, but it is worth a shot.

_Parkinson's affects everyone in a unique way.

_Plan ways to make it easier to navigate your home to better handle daily activities.

_Anything that helps you, as minor and insignificant as it may seem, can be a lifesaver.

_You are in this for the long haul, so it is vital to simplify your day.

PLANNING AHEAD...BUT FOR WHAT?

You know the old saying about the best-laid plans? If I may paraphrase, the best-laid plans are often screwed up by real life. We plan for our future with no knowledge of what we will face. Throw into this chancy scenario the diagnosis of a potentially debilitating disease, and life catches you off-guard and unprepared.

I am looking at my next birthday. Add another digit to that sixty I just celebrated. Holy cow! How did I get to be...what? So old? Sixty is not so old, anymore. What is it they say—sixty is the new forty? None of my friends looks or acts sixty. We should have many good years ahead of us. For some of us, though, life has stepped in and thrown a curveball.

My diagnosis of Parkinson's turned my world upside-down. The scary part for me now is that I already have lived with PD for eleven years. How much longer can it be held at bay? My family has the longevity gene, but who wants to live a long time with something like this, especially if it takes away your ability to function or the very essence of who you are?

I guess I do. I want to see the grandchildren I may have, live and enjoy life.

My husband and I talk about our future in an upbeat way, as though there were no barriers to what we want to do. I don't know if that is a good or a bad thing. We talk about travel, moving, where to move—but not right away. In the back of my mind, though, I always know that our plans could crash in a second. I have heard that PD is a twenty-year disease. In other words, it has a lifetime of twenty years. I am sixty-one, now. I have had PD for twelve years. I don't want to do the math.

Truly, anything can happen to anyone at any time. It doesn't have to be a medical issue. You might be called on to take care of an elderly relative or to help with grandchildren. You might get hit by a bus. We all know how precarious life can be, and yet we must plan for the rest of our lives without all the information to do so. Or, sometimes we have too much information, and yet we still make mistakes. The only thing we can do is go ahead and make our plans—and then live for today and hope our decisions are the right ones. We also can hope that the medical community makes as many strong advances in neurological issues as they have in cancer research.

You know, as I ponder this issue, I think I may have more information than I realize. When I began sharing my journey, I asked, "If you could look into a crystal ball and see your future, would you?" I still don't think I would look. As I said, I have more information than I am willing to admit; I know what the crystal ball shows me. I prefer to believe in making each day special.

Robin Roberts

Through tears of happiness, I have been watching the return of Robin Roberts to Good Morning America. As you may know, she beat her MDS (Myelodysplastic syndrome), a type of cancer that affects the blood and strikes those who are recovering from breast cancer treatment. How can life be so cruel? No doubt, Robin thought her ordeal was over, and suddenly she had to face something that challenged her resolve again.

Fortunately, Robin's condition had the hope and the history of a successful outcome. A bone marrow transplant could save her, and she received the marrow from her sister. Along with a wonderful medical team, she also had the strongest medicines of all: hope and faith, and her wonderful family. What got her through her ordeal, Robin said, was the love from her family and friends, which filled her hospital room and followed her home. Because of the prayers and faith they shared, this crisis made them all stronger. Robin believed she could fight MDS and win.

Like Robin, I have love and prayer and family and friends. I am also optimistic that my story will have a happy ending, too. What I don't have—what all of us don't have who have been given the scourge of Parkinson's or ALS or MS or Alzheimer's—is a cure. Even if not the ultimate treatment, I wish scientists could give us something to pin our hopes on, something to assure us that they are speeding forward to satisfy our lust for that cure. We need to hear something positive that we can wrap our heads and hands around.

Robin had a light at the end of her tunnel. Bone marrow transplants to fight her disease had been performed many times before with successful results. Sometimes I wonder if Parkinson's sufferers even have a tunnel!

I have some regrets about how I have coped with my disease. Unlike Robin, I never told my mother. I didn't think she could handle it. I thought I was protecting her. In reality, she was a strong woman and a very religious woman. I needed her prayers and I needed her hugs and I needed her voice to tell me everything would be all right. Instead, I kept it to myself. Now, I believe that she is praying for me in heaven. At least she is closer to God. Maybe He will listen.

PARTNERS

It is comforting to have a partner by your side as you make your way through the hills and valleys of life, someone who will pick you up when you trip over your own two feet and who will make you do your exercises even when you don't want to. Someone who can still make you laugh. Someone who still makes you catch your breath when you see him walk into a room.

In April 2015, Hubby and I will have been married for forty years. Forty years is a long time to be with one person. He has that quick Irish wit that flows off his tongue effortlessly, and he is an astute observer of life and people. Often, he is the brunt of our jokes because he can be so clueless about things that it can only be funny. It is hard to stay angry at someone who can reduce you to laughter in the middle of a heated discussion. I admit I have laughed at him at his expense, but everywhere we go, everyone who knows him loves him, and we are all happy to have him in our lives.

We met in high school. He attended an all-male Catholic school, and I attended an-all female Catholic school. We met at a mixer one Friday night. I think he was drawn to the faux leather skirt my mother had sewn for me. He always references it (read, "makes fun of it") when we talk about our first meeting.

Good thing I didn't wear the matching vest. He would have been overwhelmed. We exchanged phone numbers, and he surprised me when he called and invited me to another dance. Problem: He was seventeen and a senior, while I was just a lowly sophomore, and he had a car! My dad said no, that he would drive me to the dance, and I could meet him there. Didn't sit too well with my future hubby, but he took a chance, and the rest, as they say, is history.

We are total opposites. He is left-brained; I am right-brained. When you ask him how old someone is, he likes to give you the year they were born and expects you to do the math. He will talk to anyone. His motto is, "A stranger is a friend you haven't met, yet." Are you kidding me? As for me, I am going to sit by myself until the new friend is thoroughly vetted by the police. Didn't his mother teach him not to talk to strangers?

He loves politics. I hate politics. I love traipsing through art museums and watching romantic comedies. He falls asleep in the theater. When we watch TV, he constantly flips the channels—to find what? A war movie, no doubt, or the History Channel, or sports. I am happy with comedies and some talk shows. He would be happy to leave the news on all the time, and it is the same news every time. And shopping? Forget about it. If I am looking for a blue shirt, he picks up the first one he sees and says, "Here, I found one. Let's go."

I have a shirt that says, "Keep talking and I'll nod my head and pretend I'm listening." Get the idea?

So, now we are faced with a disease that will more than likely steal time we were supposed to have together. Parkinson's quickly extinguished everything we wanted to do. When I look at my future, everything is unclear.

I can't help but feel it is my fault that Parkinson's chose me to jump on. But, Hubby was ready to fight back, and his reaction was quick. He convinced me that we should buy a place in a warm climate, so we chose Naples, Florida. We are luckier than most. We were financially able to buy a condo in a warm climate. We have been able to see almost all of the United States and have visited many countries in Europe. We have had a wonderful life so far, and I intend it to continue for many, many years. Often, these days, I am reminded of our vows: "In sickness and health, 'til death do us part." When you are young and in love, you don't think of all that can go wrong.

He does so much for me, and he doesn't realize I know about many of them. He, who had never exercised too much in his earlier years or gone to a doctor regularly, is now a health addict. He runs, takes walks, gets regular checkups, and has reduced his unhealthy eating. I know he is doing these things for me. He needs to stay healthy in order to take care of me. And since he can't sit still, this is a good turnabout. I hope I would be as strong for him as he is for me.

Above all else, he is a good sport, and with a wife who has Parkinson's, this is a handy thing.

HOPE FLOATS

I have been feeling really good, lately, which is quite a change from a few months ago when I felt lousy. Then, my legs were weak, I had no energy, and I didn't want to do anything, but sit and read magazines, and even that was a chore! For some reason, that has changed. I have been busy and active and feeling better than I have in a long time. I tried to attribute it to something, but I haven't changed my meds. I am walking more, so maybe that is it.

Parkinson's disease is a see-saw. One day I feel really great and the next day I don't even want to move. Days like that scare me, especially when there are several in a row. I wonder if I will bounce back, if I will ever be whole again and feel like my old self.

Who knows? I must stop questioning it. Every good day is a gift. I shall enjoy each as it is given to me. I have to believe there will be a cure, soon. Some days, it is the only thing that keeps me going.

So, I shall make a mental note that, so far, I have always bounced back, and I will do it again.

Let's Get Physical

I have always exercised. I've bicycled, walked, taken classes, and so on. But, when Parkinson's hit me like a medicine ball, I found it hard to do things I once did quite easily. Again, it's the balance issue. I have solved it so far by using a cane and trading a bicycle for a three-wheeler. I have always believed in "use it or lose it," and now, with PD, I know that the most important thing I can do is to keep moving.

Accordingly, Hubby and I joined a gym. We didn't want one with all the chrome and mirrors and hard bodies walking around. If you are over fifty-five, you know what I mean. All we needed was a treadmill and a few machines for upper body strength.

Soon, I had a personal trainer! Initially, I refused, but I quickly realized I could use help to navigate the fierce looking, body-breaking machinery of the gym. I knew I should be working with a physical therapist, but I figured, since I was there, I might as well get some help. I got more than I bargained for with him, and I think he got more than he bargained for with me. At least we were starting on the same page.

His name was Justin, and he was twenty-five, my son's age; a really nice kid, and quite knowledgeable about his field. If I had been in better physical condition, it would have been fine.

Right away, of course, I told him about the PD. He had never worked with anyone who had Parkinson's; I'm not sure if he really knew what it is. Generally, you don't see PD patients working at a gym with a personal trainer, I would think. At first, he treated me like a regular. Soon, though, he realized that I wasn't your normal person who could manage all the abnormal things he wanted me to do. Like ride a bike at some unbelievable pace—not once, but three times, and for two whole minutes each time! Or stand on one foot for—how long? And balance, too?

I explained that my body was fighting me. I was pleased that he did some research and realized that PD requires balance training more than anything else. He changed the program to address my balance. The exercises were challenging.

For example, when I squatted down, it was very difficult to stand up; sometimes I fell backward in the process of trying. Since I was close to the ground, I just rolled. Nothing was broken, except my pride.

Justin pushed me as I would never push myself, and I enjoyed our sessions. For a while, I believed they were helping.

It was unfortunate that he wanted so badly for me to be whole again. He wanted me to walk with my shoulders high, my chest out, and in a straight line. I wanted that, too, but the PD prevents me from doing it. It causes my back to twist and turn in horrible ways that I can't control.

Parkinson's does things to your body that you aren't prepared for. My doc brandishes a lot of medical terminology around, words I have to consult various dictionaries to understand because the definitions are nearly as complex as the terminology. Of course, I usually don't know how to spell them, and Spell

Check is useless. I have to slow down my doctor so that I can write the terms correctly and study them when I get home. In basic English, he means that my posture is deteriorating and my spine is out of whack, and now I am waking up in the morning with a stiff neck and achy body.

I had to bid farewell to Justin, my first and only personal trainer, who earnestly tried to meet my unusual demands for exercise. Now, I'm going to physical therapy. I already know that physical therapy will be effective. The physical therapists know how the human body is supposed to work. Marilyn, my PT, has helped me already by suggesting I use a neck pillow or roll up a towel to support my neck at night. I followed her advice, experienced a refreshing night's sleep, and awoke without neck pain.

I want to be active. I don't need a hard body, but I want to develop muscles and stamina. Marilyn told me I am very strong because of the work I did at the gym. Hear that, Justin? We did good.

Good News, Bad News

The Good News: There really isn't any good news. When you have Parkinson's, you have to make your own. Recently, I did. I passed my own personal test, and that is good. Hubby went on another three-day business trip. That part was not so bad. I have stayed by myself before. When I had to drive, then, my brother was my support person. It was a victory. This time, I had to drive Hubby to and from the airport by myself. In the dark, too, and without my brother's help this time. I don't drive much because I just don't like it, so I was very anxious. The trip was all highway, all the way, and I did it! I held my own with the mammoth trucks, erratic drivers, and terrible traffic.

This second driving experience has restored my sense of independence, which I thought I had lost because of PD. I got it back, at least for a while. How long I can keep it, I don't know; but for now, I am almost the old me.

This is an example of what PD does to you. It intrudes into almost any decision you make, from scheduling a vacation to buying a major item to deciding when to sell your house. All these decisions are colored by the unknown progression of the disease, the unpredictability. All you can do is learn to manage the symptoms as they emerge to accommodate your failing body.

The bad news is that some days are really bad, and they usually start out that way. Like this morning. My bladder woke me at five a.m. Slowly, I got up, my first steps toward the bathroom tentative. I wondered whether my legs would hold me up. I never thought of such a thing before Parkinson's became part of my life. Again slowly, I make my way back and crawl into my warm bed next to a snoring hubby. I nestle down, eager to go back to sleep. Nothing. I am wide awake with no chance of sleep. My mind is too full of things I have to do. It's the best time to write and the best time to do tasks that require attention.

This is difficult to say: I am still doing well, but I see that I am failing. I do not like to admit that. Sometimes, I just need to sit and cry for a while in private. I am trying to maintain my optimism, but it is waning. I must not let that happen. I lose my balance easily. I'm using my cane more. I can feel it now when my meds begin to wear off, and I juggle my meds, trying to accommodate the changes. I'm exercising. I hope I will find other things I can do to maintain my functioning because I am becoming very afraid of what the rest of my life has in store for me.

I don't want to become someone who is weak, who can't speak for herself, who constantly clings to her spouse. I was born on Independence Day, remember? What I fear the most is losing my independence, becoming dependent.

Here is the worst news of all: I know now that I will never wake up in the morning feeling refreshed, healthy, and with a body that is ready for the day and does what I want it to. First, I have to get my energy back by taking the dreaded pills, which wear off in mid-afternoon, when I have to take the pills again.

Back to the good news: I will not give in. I will seize the day and enjoy it and believe that there will be many more. I will take the meds, do those exercises, and hope, no believe, that I will be able to maintain my independence as I grow older.

When people hear the word Parkinson's, most think of the tremors, yet there are so many more aspects of the disease that you might never know unless you are experiencing them. The simplest and perhaps the most annoying is the inability to roll over in bed. Thus, the position I fall asleep in is mine for the whole night. I can only hope that it is a comfortable one. Another symptom is happening to me right now as I write this: my fingers are on the mouse and they twitch, which sometimes causes me to click when I should have clacked, so to speak. I could lose a whole document, such as a manuscript, easily.

The meds cause my blood pressure to fall, so I get dizzy, and of course, that means I may fall—and place myself in jeopardy of broken bones. Another invisible effect of Parkinson's is that I can't compromise on safety precautions that most people rarely think of. I have to hold on to the railing when going up or down the stairs and getting in and out of the shower. Yes, everybody should be doing that, but most people have the old it-can't-happen-to-me feeling. I don't.

Hesitation or freezing when I try to walk is probably the most troubling to me. I ask my feet to move, and they don't. I only have a little bit of that, but I know people who can't move without that little push. And if you are lucky, that one little push will enable you to move more than one step. I have read that dancing or listening to music in your head helps with this, that somehow the rhythm enables the muscles to move. So, if you see me dancing along the road, you'll know what that's about.

When you have PD, your voice becomes very soft, and mine was already soft to begin with. People lean in to hear me. I try to speak up, but that ain't happening, either. Since I never liked to talk much, anyway, it is lucky that I was given the ability to write.

I find it difficult to pick up small objects, like my pills—and even my pen! At some point I may have to take classes in how to swallow and talk so I don't choke and give everyone around me a heart attack.

When my doctor switched me to Sinemet, the be-all and end-all of the drugs in his arsenal, he told me I might experience violent stomach upsets. Might experience stomach upsets? Violent upsets? I didn't worry. I have a strong stomach.

You guessed it. About an hour and a half after I took the new meds, I became horribly, violently stomach sick. My body finally got used to the new toxin, but it took almost two weeks of lying on the couch and sipping ginger ale.

The drugs are a story in their own right. These doctors are fooling around with my brain, for crying out loud. Dealing with PD is not for sissies. The drugs have to be carefully monitored and balanced and tweaked because they interact with each other uniquely and produce various side-effects. My doc warned me that one of the drugs could bring out obsessive-compulsive behavior, usually in the areas of eating, shopping, gambling, or sex. None of those effects have happened to me, yet. Other drugs cause your spine to twist so that you can't stand straight.

Hallucinations are another side-effect. My personal favorites occurred at the beginning of my treatment. Once, I awoke from a short doze on the couch to see people standing in front of me as if they belonged there. They were all dressed up, but I couldn't see their faces. I caught on fast to that particular side-effect, and the people went away. I have had terrible dreams, some so realistic that I screamed out loud. One of the first times it happened was when we were visiting in Key West. Apparently, I let out a blood-curdling scream in the middle of the night. We were with another family, and my friend jumped out of bed to make sure no one was being murdered. I didn't admit I was the one who'd let out that awful scream until much later.

Another time, my hubby was sleeping with his arms around me, and I must have been dreaming someone was trying to choke me. So I did what I was told to do in all those safety videos—I bit him on the arm that was around my neck. I still talk in my sleep, but the bad dreams have vanished. Who knows what awaits me next?

The Ugly. There are at least three ugly things PD brings, and those are the symptoms I am most afraid of: falling, bladder control, and the Mask of Parkinson's.

Falling: Because my balance is compromised, I am very afraid I will fall against something or, worse, someone, and hurt them badly. I had a two-week period when I fell several times—and this is the scary part—for no apparent reason. No here it comes, no warning—I just fell. How do you plan for that?

Bladder control: PD robs you of muscle control, and your bladder is a muscle. Need I say more?

The Mask: I do not want my face to be devoid of all expression. Someone once told once told me he could discern more from my animated face than he could from my words.

Am I strong enough to continue? I have to be. I still have not come to terms with my situation. I have not made that full circle around to accepting this monster. And I am still hopeful that someday we will have a cure. I am still hopeful that I will not have to accept that there is no cure.

I just take each day, one at a time, good, bad, or ugly. I hope for the best, but prepare for the worst.

THE TALK

It happens to us all at some point: We need to sit down with our significant other and talk about selling the house. One day, you realize that the house has gotten too big for just the two of you. The laughter and tears, the wonderful and not-so-wonderful times that once filled this house have quieted and been replaced by a calm realization that you have taken a house and made it a home. Your children have grown up and taken flight, just as you wanted them to, just as they are supposed to do. The dirty laundry on the floor and dishes in the sink have been replaced by a shiny, uncluttered countertop. Stark might be a better word.

This house talk hits at different times for different couples. My mom and dad stayed in their home until they could not be left alone anymore. When you have a disease like Parkinson's, that time is almost dictated to occur, and in my case, at all too early an age. My hubby and I have had the talk. We are not thinking of selling right now, but we are planning ahead.

In my life, I have been responsible for redistributing two households of memories. The task was bittersweet, especially when I was downsizing my mother. I uncovered beautiful valentines and anniversary cards that let me into a part of my parents' world I had never seen before: the personal notes between a husband and wife. And who was I to say what went and what stayed? They were my mother's things; what right did I have to determine their fate? Yet, she was in a nursing home when I was selling her house, and she did not have the faculties to tell me if she wanted any of them.

I came across pictures dating back to the 1930s, carefully pasted with those black corners in albums on black pages. In white pen, she carefully noted who was in the picture, where it was taken, and the year. Often there were comments on a photo: This is Mike (my father) saying hello to yet another dog he met. I found it odd to notice what mattered the most to me. It wasn't the good china or crystal I wanted, but strange things for which any level-headed person would question my sanity. One was a cracked mirror, which now hangs in my dining room. I found it in the basement near the washer, where I used to sit and watch her do laundry. I found treasures right in front of my eyes that I never knew were there.

I do not wish to burden my son with doing this task for me. As I go along, I plan to pare down the clutter in my life. Yet, I wonder—will freeing him from the task of redistributing my memories deprive him of the sweet satisfaction of discovering a different side to us, his parents?

My husband and I have had the talk. We try to anticipate our future so that we will be as ready as we can be to leave the past and embrace our future, whatever that may be. When the time comes.

The dirty laundry on the floor? You won't miss it. They always bring it with them when they come for a visit.

THE TRUMP CARD

When I was diagnosed with PD, I promised myself that I would not use Parkinson's as my trump card. You know what I mean. During a disagreement, out comes the trump card, "Well, you don't have what I have. You don't know what it is like to have Parkinson's."

In my opinion, this is hitting below the belt. So far, I have stayed away from using my challenges as an arguing point, and I promise not to. Maybe as the Parkinson's advances and I become more frustrated with being unable to do things on my own, it will be harder to keep this promise. So let me apologize to my friends and loved ones beforehand for any names I may call you. Because I certainly don't mean them. I know you are struggling as much as I am, just in a different way.

Dear Santa

I know it is too early to write to you; after all, it's not even Halloween yet. What I'm asking for may take a while, so I wanted to get my request in first:

I want to wake up feeling good. I don't want to wake up with Parkinson's anymore. I want to jump out of bed with all the energy I should have naturally and not be dependent on piles of pills to get me through the day.

I want to stop waiting for the next wheel to fall off the cart, for the next stage of this disease to make itself known. I really don't want to get into that, but the future is not pretty.

I want to maintain my mobility and brain function until I am one hundred years old.

I want to see my son married with grandchildren who will call me Babciez.

I want to stay in my home until I am ready to leave it and not be forced out by some disease I didn't invite in.

That's not such a big list, is it, Santa?

These are things I don't want you to bring:

I don't want to be a burden on anyone.

I don't want to lose any more brain cells.

I don't want people to feel sorry for me.

I don't want to hold back anyone I am traveling with, whether through life or down the street.

And Santa, I am not asking this last thing for just myself, but for everyone who shares my burden. Please, it is still early. Maybe you can bring a cure for Christmas.

Thank you, Deborah.

My Body

When you have a condition like Parkinson's, you learn to read your body and what is happening to it. So far, so good. I have been able to control new symptoms by changing meds, but I know the meds will not work for the rest of my life. It scares me. My body feels heavy, I cannot stand straight, and my feet feel like they have weights attached. Whenever I am having a "slow" day like this, I am afraid it is the beginning of the end of the meds' value. Eventually, they will be useless. So, every time they don't last as long as I believe they should, I get scared. I ask myself if this is it. Are there other things I can do, other drugs I can take to ward it off? Maybe I am trying to do too much and that is why my body isn't responding as it should. Yes, that has to be it. It is almost Christmas, and I am doing too much.

By now, I am willing to live the rest of my life with my current challenges. Is that too much to hope for?

Not knowing when Parkinson's will fully encompass me makes it very hard to plan ahead. What if we plan a vacation and when the time comes I am not able to handle the travel? Whenever a new symptom shows up, like a slight tremor of my hand, I get scared and dwell on being robbed of my future. I think of how my life "should" be. I was supposed to be enjoying my "early retirement" with travel, working on our house, and giving big holiday dinners. I should be planning for a future unencumbered by illness or disease. What went wrong?

I am on a journey that will take me…where? Not to the life I had planned for. I don't know what lies at the end of this for me. Or maybe I just can't face it right now. I can handle this, but I might need a little more help than I am willing to admit. Am I scared? Of course. I know that PD has four stages, but I can't tell you which one I am in. I don't read about them because I don't want to see in writing what will happen to me.

I realize now that my body will never be the same again. I have a special way to get out of bed in the mornings, a special way to sleep with a neck roll so my neck doesn't hurt, and special exercises to help with balance and walking. When I squat, I roll backwards. I don't like to be alone in crowds. I don't like to go to parties or weddings or any gatherings where I can be jostled and easily toppled. I need a strong arm to help me in these situations, but don't want to be a clinging, timid person. When I get up from a chair, I never know whether I will be stiff. People who know my condition watch how I get up and move, and I don't like to be watched. My appearance is shot because these drugs have a side-effect that makes my spine twist and turn in the wrong directions and leaves me with terrible back pain.

These things happened to me just as I was finally, at fifty, getting comfortable in my skin and finding a flattering hairstyle and clothes. I don't know if you can understand that. Now, the vision I have in my mind is very different from the one in the mirror.

But, let me not end on a bad note. I am still standing, still moving, still able to do whatever I want, albeit a bit slower given the issues I have. So, I still enjoy my life, my travels, my friends, and my family, and I do look forward to my future without PD and a return to my normal self.

ANOTHER NEW YEAR
WITHOUT A CURE

The start of a new year is traditionally a time to review your life and make resolutions for change. I don't do resolutions well, especially when they involve things like reducing how much I eat of my favorite food group—cookies. I believe in making a change when a change is needed, not according to the calendar.

This time of year is bittersweet for most people. I have all my wonderful memories, but not the people who made them. Suddenly, I am one of the older generation, the ones orchestrating the new memories.

Truth be told, I don't know what stage of Parkinson's I am in or what awaits me in the coming year. I haven't read in-depth about the progression of PD. I know it isn't pleasant, and I will discover it for myself in time. Now, I will celebrate the things I can still do. I can assure you that if I had not been given the eleven "free years" I have experienced, I would not be this optimistic.

After close to twelve years, my symptoms have remained manageable, and I can continue to enjoy most everything I did before. I don't know why I was given this extra time. Maybe it's because, instead of giving in to the push and pull of PD, I ignore it as best I can. And yet, that could be one of the bad things, because when it does turn into full-blown PD, it may hit me all the harder. I shake off such thoughts. Tomorrow is another story. Having a great doctor like Dr. Rathi makes a big difference.

Sure, there are things I can't do anymore. I can't rake the leaves in the fall or bend down to plant the daffodil bulbs, but I can smell the newly raked leaves and enjoy the sight of picked flowers in the spring. Most important, I have wonderful family and friends who are there to help me when I falter.

In a sense, blogging has been my therapy. Writing about my journey with PD helps me handle it somewhat. And maybe it will help someone else in the process.

I promised myself I would be open and blunt about my life. I want those who do not live with the burden of PD to realize the ways it takes over every aspect of personal and family life. I think about it twenty-four hours a day.

Happy New Year to us all, and especially to all who are suffering from the major, life-sapping illnesses. I hope by the end of another year, we will be given a cure.

A Tribute to Mom

I lost my mom less than two weeks ago as I write this, although in a sense I lost her years ago. She was almost ninety-four when she died. I knew that her life in this world was winding down, but it is still hard to lose your mother, one of the most important people in your life. And yet, as hard as it is to watch someone die, sometimes it can be even harder to watch them live. While she was often in another world, I was lucky that she always recognized me, and that was a wonderful gift.

Mom was born in 1918. Imagine the changes she has lived through over those years! From airplanes to spaceships to men landing on the moon, from the internet to Facebook and Twitter, and I can assure you she would be appalled to see what is posted for the world to see. She lived through too many wars, the Great Depression, and the World Trade Center attack. And yet, she never even learned how to drive a car.

There comes a time in the parent-child relationship when the hierarchy of the relationship changes, when the child becomes the parent. I believe that happened when my father died. They had been married for fifty-nine years. Their days were structured just so. He played the piano, and she listened from another room. They set the table for breakfast before they went to bed. When he died, she was lost without him. He was her eyes and ears. He took her everywhere. He sat in his chair in the den at night, and as she went upstairs each night, she'd look in on him to see him reading or sleeping. After his death, every time she looked and saw him gone, her heart broke even more. He wasn't there. He had been her rock, as my husband is for me, and he wasn't there.

I never told her about my Parkinson's disease. On several occasions, she spoke of a friend who'd had the disease, always preceding it with the observation that Parkinson's is the worst disease ever. So, how could I tell her I had it? I couldn't. I kept the secret from a lot of people until I knew she would never hear about it. Truly, she was the one person I most wanted to tell. Mom was extremely religious; she probably had a direct line to God. I wanted to tell her so she could pray for me, but I couldn't burden her with that knowledge.

Now, she has been reunited with my dad and her sisters, brothers, and parents. I am sure Dad greeted her with a polka played on a baby grand. She left a legacy of kindness, love, and decency. She helped anyone who needed her help, and her little part of the world was a better place because she cared. She gave me and my brother the tools to cope in this world while remaining kind and honest. I hope we pass on that legacy to her grandchildren. I think we have.

So, Mom, I love you, and I will miss you. If you have a chance to talk to the Guy in charge, tell Him about all of us struggling with these cruel diseases and ask Him to speed up the cure—if He doesn't mind.

Support Groups

Early on, my neurologist Dr. Rathi asked if I had joined a support group. Then, and I appreciate his honesty, he commented that support groups would probably depress me. He was right. At the time, I was still in the early throes of the disease and showed no major signs.

I wasn't ready to open a door that would show me my future. That would be like looking into the crystal ball, and frankly, I was still scared. This was real. This was my future, and I didn't want to see what lay ahead of me. I knew support groups could be a tremendous help and a valuable resource. They are a place you can be yourself and not hide the disease. I was afraid I would be terribly depressed to see up close what Parkinson's does to its victims: the stooped posture, the halting and faltering footsteps, and the lack of facial expression. I wasn't ready to be thrust into the realities of my situation. I already knew where the progress of the disease would leave me; it would leave me as—well, as less than the person I have always been. So, I put the idea on hold for a while.

However, I did attend a seminar concerning the treatment and progression of PD. As we walked into the room, I told Hubby that I expected to be very depressed by the time I walked out.

Well, I was wrong. I met a lot of people at different levels of PD, fighting it with different weapons. Some were into the physical with the goal to keep moving: dancing, exercise, and the like. Others were constantly researching the condition or studying nutrition or medications. With so many on our side and willing to share their thoughts, how could we not be close to an answer?

I learned a lot about PD, at times more than I wanted to know. What we all had come to find, and still do not have, was actual, wrap-your-arms-around-it hope that a real cure will be found in the near future.

Eventually, I did attend a support group meeting. Hubby and I stopped into a local office to get information for this book. The staff was very nice and told me about how they help make PD patients' lives a little easier by providing resources, doing research on various topics, and discussing alternative treatments that seem to work for some. They held luncheons and dance and swim classes. I agreed to come to the next meeting, even though I realized I didn't have to. I could have just disappeared into the night, but I decided to go back to see what I could learn. During the drive there, I got increasingly depressed and sad. As it turned out, my husband and I were the first to arrive. My eyes filled with tears as each person entered with his or her personal challenges. Some were on their own. Some were supported by a cane, a walker, or a caregiver.

The questions began as they greeted the others. "How is John? I heard he was not doing well," and, "Is Emma still in the...?" Why had I come? I didn't belong. And Hubby certainly did not feel he belonged in that caregiver category.

The leader asked each of us to tell our story. Somehow, I felt safe and was very relaxed. Each person who spoke was dealing with the disease in his or her own way. They fought it through drugs and by constantly changing the combination to address whatever symptom was worst at the time. One gentleman was trying to wean himself off all drugs and felt this was the answer for him. It was something most of us wouldn't try, but we were interested in his results. He was still experiencing the tremors and halting gait, but he wanted to cut back on the extremely strong drugs that create other side effects at times. Another gentleman had undergone deep brain stimulation and praised its results. All spoke about how important it was to keep moving and stay flexible. Some went to yoga classes. Others belonged to gyms or took dancing lessons. I used to love to dance, not the free-form kind where you just move your body in time to the music, but the beautiful footsteps of a waltz or a cha-cha. Being reminded gave me the incentive to take some dancing classes.

Most important was seeing people with the same disease I have, and they were surviving and taking control of their lives. Listening to others speak, I saw that we all reacted to this PD blip on our radar screen in much the same ways. Some, like me, hid their disease because of outside circumstances, feeling they had to protect their jobs or families from the consequences of their having PD. Many talked about the falls they had taken, and others had suggestions on how to avoid future falls.

It was interesting that many used terms like "coming out of the closet with the diagnosis." Many struggled with accepting help. Like me, most had been caregivers and hated to admit that now they were the ones needing help.

I was surprised that I wanted the meeting to last longer so I could ask questions and bask in the resiliency of the wonderful people I'd met. It was very encouraging to talk to people who were managing, people who were not letting PD stop them.

I expect to return at some point to get to know my new friends better.

There was one sour note. A woman came up to me after the meeting and asked, "Well, what is it like to see your future?"

How cruel. And how sad for her.

How You Can Help Someone with Parkinson's Disease

Friends and loved ones are more than happy to provide what you need, especially initially. Soon, though, you may be moved to the back burner, not because they don't care anymore, but because they have their own issues. Let's be honest: we are all guilty, myself included, of saying, "Let me help," or, "Tell me what you need," and not following up on that offer. Most people truly want to help in any way they can, but they do not know what to offer you unless you tell them exactly what you need. So, let's start at the beginning.

When I tell you about my diagnosis of Parkinson's—and I mean this in a loving way—just shut up.

I don't need to hear about your friend who died from a fall down the stairs because of Parkinson's or your uncle who has dementia and is currently in a nursing home and will probably spend the rest of his life there because of Parkinson's. I don't need you to tell me how horrible a disease it is. Don't you realize I already know what this disease is going to do to me? Why do you have to point out what I already know? Would you speak to someone recently diagnosed with cancer about how horrible cancer is?

Why not say something positive, even if you have to lie? Tell me about the wonderful research you know is taking place. Make a donation to any of the nonprofits set up to look for answers to Parkinson's disease, most notably The Michael J. Fox Foundation for Parkinson's Research. That is what I and all of us who have been diagnosed with PD need—not a heavy dose of reality, but handfuls of hope.

I was always a very independent person, not seeking or taking anyone's help, but this is probably going to be bigger than I even want to imagine. You can be helpful by keeping the following in mind.

I think most PD patients want to be included in what is happening in their friends' lives and in life in general. I have heard from others with Parkinson's that at times it is just too difficult to be in a social setting. I can already understand the great physical tiredness that comes over you. It is deafening in its nature and intensity. What would be helpful in this regard is your acceptance and your understanding when I say no to your invitations. Sometimes, I just can't handle the environment a social engagement will place me in. However, it does not mean I don't want to spend time with you.

Little things are what matter the most. Gestures made subtly and with thought are welcome, especially when I venture out in public. Gestures like taking my arm when we are in a crowd or getting something from the buffet table for me so I don't have to endure people's looks when I walk across the room. Just be attentive, but don't make a big fuss. On a practical note, when you give me a hug, be careful not to squeeze too hard. You might throw me off-balance, so that I topple over and take you down with me.

Most important, I want my loved ones and friends to promise they will watch out for Hubby as time goes on. He is the one who will take the brunt of my anger and frustration, who must deal with the tears and angry words that I am likely to have. Those who love us the most will be the ones who get to see the ugly side of Parkinson's. The ugly side of me. I want to know that Hubby will continue to stay involved in his interests. I don't want him to be burdened by me 24/7. He has to enjoy his life so I can enjoy—or maybe a more apt word here is *endure*—mine.

Caregivers

Caregivers. I hope God holds a special place in heaven for them. They are exhausted, frustrated, overworked, alone, sad, and scared. Often, the very person they are caring for yells at them. I am sure they remind themselves of the "in sickness and in health" part of their vows frequently. How many people just walk away? How many people cannot handle the burdens of caring for someone 24/7?

Those of us who have been diagnosed with PD want to take care of ourselves for as long as we can, but usually there is a point when we cannot do it alone anymore. We need to let go of the attempt to control and do what's best for everyone involved, including ourselves. A husband I know is taking care of his wife, who has Alzheimer's. I have seen him quite angry over some little thing she has done or for asking the same question for the thirty-third time. However, he is not really angry. He is frustrated, frustrated because he is losing his life partner. He doesn't like to see her being taken from him, inch by inch. He is afraid that at some point he will be completely unable to care for her, and then what? The more we love someone, the more frustrating it is.

When my mom was in a nursing home, there was a woman there who had suffered a stroke. She was in her eighties, and her husband was older. Every day, he came to visit at exactly three p.m. She expected him every day at three p.m. If he wasn't there every day at three p.m., everyone heard about it. He always brought her some lunch or a sweet treat and stayed until visitors were asked to leave. Clearly, he still loved her, and he cared for her as best he could. His whole life was wrapped up in her and keeping her comfortable and happy. He brought her dolls and singing-and-dancing windup toys.

He had been doing this for years, even though she often hollered at him or dropped the F bomb, which actually was quite funny because you just knew she probably never used that word before the stroke. I am pretty sure she would be appalled if she realized what she was saying. Her poor husband, apologetic and embarrassed, would try to calm her down.

All of us will likely be called on to be caregivers at some point in our lives. I know that some people just can't do it, cannot visit a hospital or nursing home. I can understand this; it is not pleasant to spend afternoons visiting friends or relatives. When I visited Mom in the nursing home, knowing I have Parkinson's made it all the worse. I'd watch all the residents, identify those with Parkinson's, and realize that their fate might be mine. I often came home in tears that I could be one of them. And like everyone, I don't want my family to suffer because of what is happening to me.

I Don't Want to Be
an Afterthought

Doctors have identified a continuum of emotions that people experience when they get really bad news. The first is denial of the situation, followed by anger, depression, and despair until coming to acceptance. I am nowhere near acceptance. I don't know whether that is a good thing or a bad thing. When my brain finally runs out of that dopamine stuff and can no longer tell my body what to do, it's gonna hit me hard. It is possible that I will be prepared for it. Somehow, I don't think so. The other question is whether my family and friends will be ready to accept it. I don't think they will.

I don't like to be broken. I don't like to be a damaged person. But, most of all I don't want to be referenced in a conversation as an afterthought, as in, "Oh, yes, how is Deborah? I heard she wasn't doing well," and then they get on with their own lives. I do not begrudge them being able to go out and play. I don't. I just want to remain a real person in their lives, and not just an afterthought. I don't like to admit this, especially to my closest family and friends. I want them to have happy lives, free from worry about me. I guess I appear so optimistic because I have to be. I think my family and friends need to believe my optimism is justified more than I do.

LIES I TELL MYSELF

There are lies we tell ourselves because they make us feel better. We do not want to face the realities of life, and we want to protect our loved ones.

I must be a good liar, because I really believed my own fabrications. I believed that I looked the same as I always did. I believed that I was getting really good at hiding the Parkinson's. I had hidden it for ten years, and not too many knew I had it. I believed there was no twisting spine, no hesitation in walking, and no tremors.

It wasn't until after ten years that people began to say they knew something was wrong with me. "The last time I saw you, you looked so tired and sad." People don't venture to say this unless I am feeling and looking good, and I was surprised that I hadn't been fooling anyone.

When I fell, I told myself it could have been due to the unevenness of the walkway—or it could have been the PD or an untied shoelace. Tons of people trip on their shoelaces. But, wait. Have I ever tripped before? No.

When I choked on my pills, I told myself it probably happened because I took too many at once—or it could have been the PD.

When I dropped a whole carton of milk, I told myself it was probably because my hands were wet and greasy—or it could have been the PD.

The person you must always be honest with is yourself, or you will never get the proper treatment. You also can't lie to your doctor. Dr. Rathi can tell when I am…well…let's calling it withholding the truth a little bit. I'm not a good liar. As the disease progresses, undoubtedly there will be embarrassing issues I must discuss with him. I usually just blurt out my latest symptom and get it over with. Lately, I have found it more effective to write down in advance what I have to communicate. I do this in a quiet place before my appointment so I make sure to give him the information he needs to help me. Whether it is a new symptom, questions about my meds, or questions about the future of the disease, if he has the questions in writing, he can review them, and I will have communicated honestly and thoroughly.

Religion and Prayer

Several times, I have referenced religion or prayer, but more as an aside. Religion is a very personal topic to write about, and in no way would I attempt to convert you to my beliefs. I was raised in the Roman Catholic Church by a mother who was very religious and a father whose belief was quiet.

I believe in prayer, but not in the formal sense, like saying the Our Father. Memorized, standard prayers are fine for whenever you need God's ear quickly, but the form of prayer I prefer is meditating or just being aware of the beauty around me. I believe that appreciating beauty and being thankful to God is a form of prayer. Going to church isn't what makes us good people.

When first confronted with a life-altering situation, many of us ask God, "Why me?" We will never have that answer unless we believe we were given this bad news for the purpose of making something wrong, right. The truth is, I need a miracle, and I don't know how to pray for one. Is there a set of prayers? My mom used to say novenas for what she wanted. I have seen notes in the newspapers giving thanks to God for fulfilling a request. As far as I can see, miracles are rare. Maybe I don't have enough faith that they can be real. Sometimes, it seems there could never be enough prayers for what I want. Maybe I could start with a small miracle.

I am reminded of that picture and verse about footprints on the beach, which lets us know that God doesn't give us more than we can handle. Only one set of footprints doesn't mean we are alone; it means that God is carrying us. Nice thought. I hope it is true, because I am going to need a lot of carrying.

AND SO IT GOES

I started writing to examine the emotional and psychological journey experienced by someone with Parkinson's. At first, I was hopeful when the doctors told me it was only a matter of time before they found a cure. They even gave me a ballpark date—five to ten years out, they expected victory in what now seems like a losing battle. I remain hopeful and committed that a new way of treating Parkinson's disease will be uncovered soon.

I wanted this book to be balanced, and not just all optimism or all despair. I wanted it to be real. So, I guess this is my reality. I thought that I would be much more affected by the disease by now and looking for heavy-duty canes and a wheelchair. If you have Parkinson's, please don't look at me and see that after a dozen years I am able to do more than the average person with PD. Remember, the disease treats everyone differently.

How do we accept the ravages of PD or any life-stealing condition? How do we accept the fact that the disease will steal our bodies and our very being? I have no answers. Even after living with this disease for over a decade, I can't quite come to accept that it will ravage my life. Am I scared? Of course I am. But, if I think about it too much, I get depressed, and that is exactly what I don't want. I am truly an optimist, but PD may cure me of that.

So, how do I feel? Hopeful? Yes. Also drained, sore, stiff, tired, and weary. I don't like to use these negatives, but there they are, constantly on my mind. I think the best way to describe me at this point is numb. I am pretty calm about it, and I expect my doc to have something new up his sleeve when I need it. (No pressure, Dr. Rathi!) Before my diagnosis, I thought I would not be able to handle it if something like this hit me. I know that over the next few years, this thing will take its toll, and I will shed many tears. Right now, I take it day by day. Some days are better than others, and I wait and use those days for all they are worth.

I still enjoy many good days on which I can garden, paint, and write. I don't know when they will come to an end. My birthday, which is coming up shortly, is a benchmark by which I evaluate my present self against my former self. I think I did pretty well this past year. No major bumps in the road, and I hope to keep it that way.

I want so badly to hear about any discovery that would make the hunt for a cure palpable. Every so often, I hear a blurb on TV that starts out, "Researchers have found a new treatment for…" and in that split second I think maybe this time they are talking about Parkinson's—but they never are.

I am concerned about some new symptoms I am experiencing. In a sense, my life with PD may just be starting. I have no idea how bad it will get, and I don't care to look into my crystal ball any more than I already have. I hoped I would never have to write these words or say them out loud, but the disease is getting a firmer hold on me and is taking a greater toll than before. I must be losing more brain cells, because now I can feel the PD attacking my arms, at times making them feel as weighty and heavy as my legs. When I wake up in the mornings, I can feel my arms tingling. When I make a fist, it is not as strong as it used to be. But, give me a few minutes, and it comes back. The pills, which used to last for six hours, start cutting out after about three-and-a-half. Sometimes, I am so physically exhausted that I just sit here, doing nothing, but staring into space. My paints are nearby, but I don't have the strength or desire to reach for them.

The rhythm of my day is the same. I awake too early, get out of bed in the manner the physical therapists taught me, and stand. If I can move my legs to get to the bathroom, I am good to go. I take my first pills around eight a.m. Mornings are my best time of day to accomplish what I want to do that day. I know I probably do too much. Around two p.m. is time for another round of pills. Right after lunch, these days, my body starts telling me it is time for the second round; I try to hold off for as long as possible if I have something unusual to do that night. They don't seem to work as well when I wait too long to take them, and my energy falls off the radar screen. Usually, I need to sit or lie down for a while, and my energy comes back later that afternoon.

Evenings are mostly okay, but right before I should go to bed, I usually get another burst of energy and find I don't get under the covers until after midnight. Some nights, I lie in bed with no sleep until after four a.m. I know I haven't slept because our grandfather clock chimes every quarter hour, and I count them all.

Endings...and Beginnings

I had hoped I could end my story as any good story ends: you know, "And she lived happily ever after." But, I saw enough in that crystal ball to know that not every story has a happy ending. Is mine included among those?

Therefore, I will write my last chapter not as an ending, but as the beginning of a new and hopefully exciting life—albeit one I did not plan.

My life will be undergoing some major changes in the months ahead; some are a result of the PD; others are just a result of living and getting older and perhaps wiser. The men in my life precipitated the major changes. My husband hates the cold, and our son is ready to pursue other opportunities. So, it is goodbye to Boston and North Haven, Connecticut, and hello to sunny Naples, Florida.

While my new life will not be fully realized for a few years, the planning and incessant talking about the future has begun. I will begin this new life with mixed emotions. I am sad for all the people and things I will be leaving behind. And I am sorry if Hubby feels like I don't want to make these changes. I don't want to make them. Yet, things can't stay the same forever. Now, my crystal ball is whispering that moving to a more temperate climate is the wisest decision we can make, especially with Parkinson's breathing down my neck. I believe the cold weather makes my bones ache all the more. And do I really have a choice? Hubby is the one who will be bearing the burden and consequences of my affliction, so I see that the PD will be making my decisions for me.

On a practical side, where do we put all the stuff we have saved all these years: old furniture waiting for the kids' new house, old toys and records that will be worth a fortune in a few years? Well, the furniture they do not want and the records are still a dime a dozen, and holding on to this stuff is totally impractical.

I guess I am too sentimental. I'm clinging to a life I am not going to have. I don't want to sell my house this early in my life. I want many more years here. I am comfortable in this house, regardless of the stairs, but I have observed the following: where I see a home, Hubby sees a house, a structure. I see children playing in the pool, band practices, and holiday dinners. I see many more years of making memories. Hubby sees grass to cut and snow to shovel. He worries that I will slip and fall on the ice and snow. Even spending winters in Florida leaves us with the burden of taking care of a house in the Northeast during the winter. Yes, undoubtedly Hubby believes he is doing what is best for me by giving us a simpler life. I guess we both have to compromise a bit, but this is a huge and unexpected change. I will be leaving my home of almost forty years and friends of even longer. We will meet new people, I know, but it takes a long time to cultivate new, true friends. I have often thought that men don't have the deep friendships that women have. I have always been comfortable asking my women friends for an arm to steady me, and often one is offered before I know I need it. Women friends provide each other with a place just to talk without me having to open up my whole life history. My friends and I know each other's families and circumstances. We do not hesitate to rush over and offer help or just a shoulder to cry on when the bad times come. I know we will make new friends, but it is not the same. Some people may care about you as a person, but most want to carry on with their own lives and not be reminded of what they might see if they looked into their own crystal ball.

I will miss the fall colors made brilliant against the purple sky of autumn. This year, the colors were spectacular. I will miss the fluffy-white snow and being holed up for days baking cookies while the snows accumulate. And in the spring, the daffodils. Oh, the daffodils!

I will have to put together a new team of medical people to handle all the baggage I bring with me. I like my present doctors and have spent many years in their waiting rooms, sure to get excellent medical care. I trust them and can call them anytime. It will take time to establish such trust anew.

On a positive note, my family is nearby in Florida: my brother, his wife, and my nephew. The living seems easier, but I haven't yet experienced a Florida summer.

I take with me to my new home a lifetime of memories, and they will have to last me a lifetime. The world has gotten much smaller, so to speak, and almost anyone can jump on a plane and be almost anywhere in the world in a few hours. But, we cannot be down the street in ten minutes when a friend calls us to come over for pizza.

After speaking with people who have already made the change, I have discovered that people leave their homes for many reasons: to escape bad memories, to lose people they no longer want involved in their lives, to find new beginnings, to make life easier—and sometimes to lie to themselves that this change will be okay.

It Ain't Over 'Til It's Over

Throughout these pages, I have said that hope is the greatest and strongest medicine there is. I have never accepted my diagnosis. I should clarify that: while I believe I have Parkinson's, I don't believe the disease will affect me any more than it has already. I believe that I am someone special. Then, I wake up in the morning with my hands twitching. They return to normal quickly, and still I don't believe it will get any worse. This is strong denial. I don't think I will ever get past that part to total acceptance. For me to sit back and accept this diagnosis without a fight would be giving up. In our never-ending quest for a cure, those of us with life-threatening illnesses allow ourselves to become human guinea pigs; we take toxic medications that have myriad side effects, all in the name of scientific research, and all in the name of looking for a cure.

I thought I had written the last chapter, but then I was introduced to two wonderful, caring, and knowledgeable young women and the LSVT® BIG program, an evidence-based treatment approach for individuals with Parkinson's disease and other neurological disorders. I have not been wrong to hope. Hope is one of the strongest meds around. There is something I can do now that may help me live with Parkinson's disease and eventually defeat it, something I can finally wrap my head and arms around.

During my last visit, Dr. Rathi asked me if I would be interested in a program in which a certified LSVT® BIG therapist would come to my home for four consecutive days a week over four weeks to introduce me to exercises I must do twice a day. I would have to do my "homework" over the three days the therapist was not there. If I didn't meet all that was required of me, I would be kicked out of the program. I said I might be interested and to tell me more, but you know how quickly the subject changes in a doctor's office, and we moved on to another topic. Halfway down the hallway on my way out, I remembered I should go back and find out more, but I figured it would just be the same old, same old, and I forgot about it.

A few days later, I received a call from the Masonicare group telling me that Dr. Rathi had referred me to the program. The results have been outstanding. Research discovered that when someone severs his spinal cord, new synapses or connections can be created in the brain by intensive repetition of the function you want to regain. By way of example, they told me about a man whose hands trembled so much that he was embarrassed to take his wallet out of his pocket in public and take out the bills. The therapists worked with him four times a week for four weeks, and eventually he was able to take his wallet from his pocket without tremors. Others in the program became able to button up a shirt in half the time it had taken before. The program may be a lifelong commitment to perform the exercises every day, and I'm sure it is not for everyone, but it is for me. I signed on immediately. If nothing else, this new therapy renewed my hope that Parkinson's disease will eventually be tamed into submission, one way or another.

Enter Marla and Carrie, two wonderful individuals who gave me back my life. And that is truly what I feel. I finally feel like I have control of the disease, not the other way around. I feel empowered. I feel steady on my feet.

Marla and Carrie told me what I have known since my glimpses into the crystal ball, that victims of PD lose interest in everything. Our world as well as our movements, become very small, and we have no desire to do anything, or if we have the desire, we don't have the strength (or functional endurance). Through the BIG program, we retrain our brains to meet our challenges.

They assessed my abilities and limitations, and created an individualized program that showed results almost immediately. It consisted of seven specific exercises, which are protocol-based, five individualized one-step functional tasks, two more individualized advanced tasks, and what they call BIG Walking. The one thing that truly amazed me was regaining the clarity of my handwriting, which had deteriorated terribly. I was embarrassed to write down even a simple reminder because I couldn't read it later. With a few simple flicks of my hand, my old handwriting returned. Immediately! I was stunned. Marla and Carrie created other exercises to improve my balance, to help me get up gracefully and easily from a chair, how to walk and change directions without tripping over my own two feet, and how to roll over in bed. These are things we all take for granted. And for the first time in a long time, I took the car out of the garage, left Hubby home, and went shopping by myself.

I don't know how long these exercises will work. They are not stopping the progression of the disease, but they do have the ability to drastically slow it down. They are giving us a fighting chance, and most important, I feel that they gave me back my life. I feel empowered and in control because of something as simple as what amounts to non-strenuous, simple exercises. The exercises are not difficult and don't take much time. There is a protocol on the manner and order in which you do them.

If something this simple works and we can live comfortably with this disease, what a wonderful world that would be! I hope this will open a new world of treatment options.

At the beginning of the book, I asked if you would look into a crystal ball if it could foretell your future and the answer might not be pretty and you could not change it. I said no, I wouldn't look, and I still hold true to that sentiment. I just have to take each day as it comes. With all the information in the world, we still cannot plan our lives to assure our happiness.

I hope I have given anyone struggling with Parkinson's the strength to deal with this disease. We are all fighting the same demons, and not just Parkinson's sufferers, but every person alive. No one can ensure a future without hardships. At the same time, each of us with Parkinson's is unique, and the disease affects us all differently. So, do not compare yourself to me or to anyone else. Instead, here are a few suggestions I have gathered:

_Do try to get out every day.

_Don't lose touch with friends.

_Take a chance on a vacation.

_Start a new hobby.

_Research and write your family history and give it to everyone for Christmas.

I hope you will get out there and try. You know those frozen steps we sometimes experience? The ones where we need a little push to get started? Sometimes we need to give life the same little push.

AFTERTHOUGHTS

The trouble with writing or painting is that we don't know when to stop. Just a little more color here, an extra paragraph there, and it is easy to mess up your masterpiece. As I read the final chapters of my book, I think of so much more to write about. The PD is constantly changing, sometimes for the bad, yet, incredibly, sometimes for the good. So, let's try this again: How do I really feel?

I am tired, both physically and mentally. I am tired of not sleeping well, of looking at the clock every half hour and trying to decide if I should get out of bed...to do what at three a.m. in the morning? I am tired of all the pills I take to help me get through the day. I am tired of not feeling attractive anymore. I am tired of waking up in the morning and taking those first tentative steps, not knowing if this will be the day my legs give out. I am tired of doctor visits and shots and stiff necks. I am tired of crying my eyes out in the shower. I am tired of the process of moving and trying to find a place for my stuff. I am tired of watching people pass me by, either physically or mentally. I am tired of making believe this will go away any time soon, that I will not have this for the rest of my life. I am tired of being tired, of not doing what I want to do. I am tired of having a stiff body and painful back.

I am tired of being afraid of this disease, of not knowing when the next stage will come for me.

Having read this over, I am just plain tired and angry. In the end, I know I will be fine. I have too much to live for; too many people I have to take care of; too many people I love and who love me, even with this burden I am placing upon them. Sometimes, I just have to cry. It doesn't change anything, but it allows the hurt and frustration to drain away enough that I may feel better for a little while.

So, what have I learned on my journey with this disease? I have learned that, yes, it is true that we should treasure and enjoy every day, that a serious illness causes us to view each day as special. I have learned the importance of telling those we love how special they are to us, that there are many more sunsets to watch and sunrises to dream on, to give us hope that someday we will be able to start our days without this burden of Parkinson's. We need to stay healthy and focused for when that day arrives.

Life.

To be continued.

And so it goes.

Acknowledgements

Well, I actually did it—accomplished a goal I set for myself in kindergarten when I saw those yellow papers with their blue lines holding sentences that formed stories. I wanted to be a writer and write a book.

So, here I sit with it completed. My masterpiece. My baby.

Both up front and behind the scenes, many people helped me to make this a better book than I could have done on my own.

First, I want to thank my editor, Sarah Aschenbach, for asking the tough questions that allowed me to probe deeper into my heart and soul, and offer more insight and impact than I could have imagined.

I must thank all my girlfriends in my Girl's Night Out group, who, by their very presence in my life, made this book possible, just as they always try to make my life easier. They do not know how they pushed me along and made sure I finished this project with their constant questions about when it would be finished. I couldn't let them down.

A special thanks to Timothy McIntyre, who completed his literary journey before me and shared his experiences. It made my life so much easier.

Dr. Sanjay Rathi, my brilliant neurologist, has kept my body and mind strong despite the injustices inflicted by Parkinson's throughout the twelve years since I was diagnosed. Keep up the good work, Dr Rathi. It ain't over 'til it's over.

Of course, I could not have done this without the help and support of my husband, Bernie. He is my rock. He was there to catch me when I fell and stand me upright, and give me that little push to keep me going when I wanted to stop.

And to my wonderful son, Ryan—you are my world and, in a way, I wrote this book for you. Never give up on your dreams. Your road may take you in a different direction from what you expect, but if you want something badly enough, your dreams will come true.

And so it goes.

About the Author

Deborah Wilton McLoughlin grew up in New Haven, Connecticut. After meeting in high school and marrying after college, she and her husband Bernie moved to North Haven, Connecticut, where they raised their son and planned to live happily ever after. A diagnosis of Parkinson's came in 2002 when Deborah was forty-nine years old. It was a diagnosis that turned her world upside-down. Earlier, she had been employed as a human resources specialist at the Southern New England Telephone Company, and when her son was born, she chose to leave her job and stay home with him. After Deborah and her husband survived a serious car crash, they helped found the Connecticut State Chapter of Mothers Against Drunk Driving (MADD), where she served as senior accounts coordinator. She also spoke before groups of high school students to warn them about the dangers of drinking and driving.

Deborah received an associate's degree in journalism, a bachelor's degree summa cum laude in business marketing, and an MBA, all from the University of New Haven. She also is an accomplished watercolorist. She and her husband Bernie have a grown son. They are currently in the process of moving to Naples, Florida.

Morning

Waiting

Lattice with Roses

Study Fruit and Flower

Lighthouse and Barn

My Buoys

Boats. Work in progress

Botanical Gardens, Naples, FL 2015

Boston with Ryan, 2015